Utah Rules of Evidence 2018

ARTICLE I GENERAL PROVISIONS

RULE 101. SCOPE; DEFINITIONS

RULE 102. PURPOSE

Table of Contents

Rule 103. Rulings on Evidence

Rule 104. Preliminary Questions

Rule 105.   Limiting Evidence That Is Not Admissible Against Other Parties or for Other

Purposes

Rule 106. Remainder of or Related Writings or Recorded Statements

ARTICLE II JUDICIAL NOTICE

Rule 201. Judicial Notice of Adjudicative Facts

ARTICLE III PRESUMPTIONS

Rule 301. Presumptions in Civil Cases Generally

Rule 302. Applying Federal Law to Presumptions in Civil Cases

ARTICLE IV RELEVANCY AND ITS LIMITS

Rule 401. Test for Relevant Evidence

Rule 402. General Admissibility of Relevant Evidence

Rule 403.   Excluding Relevant Evidence for Prejudice, Confusion, Waste of Time, or Other

Reasons

Rule 404. Character Evidence; Crimes or Other Acts

Rule 405. Methods of Proving Character

Rule 406. Habit; Routine Practice

Rule 407. Subsequent Remedial Measures

ARTICLE V PRIVILEGES

ARTICLE VI WITNESSES

Article I General Provisions

Rule 101. Scope; Definitions

(a)   Scope. These rules apply to proceedings in Utah courts. The specific courts and proceedings to which the rules apply, along with exceptions, are set out in Rule 1101.

(b)   Definitions. In these rules:

(1)   "civil case" means a civil action or proceeding;

(2)   "criminal case" includes a criminal proceeding;

(3)   "public office" includes a public agency;

(4)   "record" includes a memorandum, report, or data compilation;

7

(5)   a reference to any kind of written material or any other medium includes electronically stored information.

2011 Advisory Committee Note. – The language of this rule has been amended as part of the restyling of the Evidence Rules to make them more easily understood and to make style and terminology consistent throughout the rules. These changes are intended to be stylistic only. There is no intent to change any result in any ruling on evidence admissibility.

ADVISORY COMMITTEE NOTE

Adapted from Rule 101, Uniform Rules of Evidence (1974). Rule 1101 contains exceptions dealing with preliminary questions of fact, grand jury proceedings, miscellaneous judicial or quasi-judicial proceedings and summary contempt proceedings. Rule 101 and 1101 are comparable to Rule 2 of the Utah Rules of Evidence (1971), except that Rule 2 made applicable other procedural rules (i.e., civil/criminal) or applicable statutes to the extent that they relax the Rules of Evidence. In addition, Rule 2 of the Utah Rules of Evidence (1971) expressly made the rules applicable to both civil and criminal proceedings.

Rule 101 adopts a general policy making the Rules of Evidence applicable in all instances in courts of the state including situations previously governed by statute, except to the extent that specific statutory provisions are expressly retained. Rule 101 also rejects Lopes v. Lopes, 30 Utah 2d 393, 518 P.2d 687 (1974) to the extent that it permits ad hoc development of special rules of court inconsistent with these Rules of Evidence.

The position of the court in State v. Hansen, 588 P.2d 164 (Utah 1978) that statutory provisions of evidence law inconsistent with the rules will take precedence is rejected.

Rule 102. Purpose

These rules should be construed so as to administer every proceeding fairly, eliminate unjustifiable expense and delay, and promote the development of evidence law, to the end of ascertaining the truth and securing a just determination.

2011 Advisory Committee Note. – The language of this rule has been amended as part of the restyling of the Evidence Rules to make them more easily understood and to make style and terminology consistent throughout the rules. These changes are intended to be stylistic only. There is no intent to change any result in any ruling on evidence admissibility. This rule is the federal rule, verbatim.

ADVISORY COMMITTEE NOTE

Rule 102 is the federal rule, verbatim, and is an adjuration as to the purpose of the Rules of Evidence.

Rule 103. Rulings on Evidence

(a) **Preserving a Claim of Error.** A party may claim error in a ruling to admit or exclude evidence only if the error affects a substantial right of the party and:

    (1) if the ruling admits evidence, a party, on the record:

        (A) timely objects or moves to strike; and

        (B) states the specific ground, unless it was apparent from the context; or

    (2) if the ruling excludes evidence, a party informs the court of its substance by an offer of proof, unless the substance was apparent from the context.

(b) **Not Needing to Renew an Objection or Offer of Proof.** Once the court rules definitively on the record — either before or at trial — a party need not renew an objection or offer of proof to preserve a claim of error for appeal.

(c) **Court's Statement About the Ruling; Directing an Offer of Proof.** The court may make any statement about the character or form of the evidence, the objection made, and the ruling. The court may direct that an offer of proof be made in question-and-answer form.

(d) **Preventing the Jury from Hearing Inadmissible Evidence.** To the extent practicable, the court must conduct a jury trial so that inadmissible evidence is not suggested to the jury by any means.

(e) **Taking Notice of Plain Error.** A court may take notice of a plain error affecting a substantial right, even if the claim of error was not properly preserved.

2011 Advisory Committee Note. – The language of this rule has been amended as part of the restyling of the Evidence Rules to make them more easily understood and to make style and terminology consistent throughout the rules. These changes are intended to be stylistic only. There is no intent to change any result in any ruling on evidence admissibility. This rule is the federal rule, verbatim.

ADVISORY COMMITTEE NOTE

This rule is the federal rule, verbatim. The 2001 amendment adopts changes made in Federal Rule of Evidence 103(a) effective December 1, 2000.

Rule 104. Preliminary Questions

(a) **In General.** The court must decide any preliminary question about whether a witness is qualified, a privilege exists, or evidence is admissible. In so deciding, the court is not bound by evidence rules, except those on privilege.

(b) Relevance That Depends on a Fact. When the relevance of evidence depends on whether a fact exists, proof must be introduced sufficient to support a finding that the fact does exist. The court may admit the proposed evidence on the condition that the proof be introduced later.

(c) Conducting a Hearing So That the Jury Cannot Hear It. The court must conduct any hearing on a preliminary question so that the jury cannot hear it if:

    (1) the hearing involves the admissibility of a confession;

    (2) a defendant in a criminal case is a witness and so requests; or

    (3) justice so requires.

(d) Cross-Examining a Defendant in a Criminal Case. By testifying on a preliminary question, a defendant in a criminal case does not become subject to cross-examination on other issues in the case.

(e) Evidence Relevant to Weight and Credibility. This rule does not limit a party's right to introduce before the jury evidence that is relevant to the weight or credibility of other evidence.

2011 Advisory Committee Note. – The language of this rule has been amended as part of the restyling of the Evidence Rules to make them more easily understood and to make style and terminology consistent throughout the rules. These changes are intended to be stylistic only. There is no intent to change any result in any ruling on evidence admissibility. This rule is the federal rule, verbatim.

ADVISORY COMMITTEE NOTE

This provision is the federal rule, verbatim, and is comparable to Rule 8, Utah Rules of Evidence (1971). Rule 104(c) recognizes that hearings on motions to suppress confessions should be conducted out of the hearing of the jury where there is a contested issue. State v. Allen, 29 Utah 2d 88, 505 P.2d 302 (1973). See also Jackson v. Denno, 378 U.S. 368 (1964). Cf. Pinto v. Pierce, 389 U.S. 31, 88 S. Ct. 192, 19 L. Ed. 2d 31 (1967).

Rule 105.   Limiting Evidence That Is Not Admissible Against Other Parties or for Other Purposes

If the court admits evidence that is admissible against a party or for a purpose — but not against another party or for another purpose — the court, on timely request, must restrict the evidence to its proper scope and instruct the jury accordingly.

2011 Advisory Committee Note. – The language of this rule has been amended as part of the restyling of the Evidence Rules to make them more easily understood and to make style and terminology consistent throughout the rules. These changes are intended to be stylistic only. There is no intent to change any result in any ruling on evidence admissibility. This rule is the federal rule, verbatim.

ADVISORY COMMITTEE NOTE

This provision is the federal rule, verbatim, and is comparable to Rule 6, Utah Rules of Evidence (1971). This rule is to be read in conjunction with Rule 20(b), Utah Rules of Civil Procedure, concerning separate trials and Utah Code Annotated, Section 77-8a-1 (1953) concerning severance, and with the caveat that a limiting instruction may be illusory at best, particularly in a complex trial or one in which the evidence substantially consists of inferences, presumptions or circumstantial evidence. The danger of prejudice may also be greater in criminal cases, where life and liberty may be at stake. Cf. Kotteakos v. United States, 328 U.S. 750, 762-63 (1946). See also Terry v. Z.C.M.I., 605 P.2d 314 (Utah 1979). The matter is addressed to the discretion of the trial judge.

Rule 106. Remainder of or Related Writings or Recorded Statements

If a party introduces all or part of a writing or recorded statement, an adverse party may require the introduction, at that time, of any other part — or any other writing or recorded statement — that in fairness ought to be considered at the same time.

2011 Advisory Committee Note. – The language of this rule has been amended as part of the restyling of the Evidence Rules to make them more easily understood and to make style and terminology consistent throughout the rules. These changes are intended to be stylistic only. There is no intent to change any result in any ruling on evidence admissibility. This rule is the federal rule, verbatim.

ADVISORY COMMITTEE NOTE

This rule is the federal rule, verbatim. Utah Rules of Evidence (1971) was not as specific, but Rule 106 is otherwise in accord with Utah practice.

Article II Judicial Notice

Rule 201. Judicial Notice of Adjudicative Facts

(a) **Scope.** This rule governs judicial notice of an adjudicative fact only, not a legislative fact.

(b) **Kinds of Facts That May Be Judicially Noticed.** The court may judicially notice a fact that is not subject to reasonable dispute because it:

   (1) is generally known within the trial court's territorial jurisdiction; or

   (2) can be accurately and readily determined from sources whose accuracy cannot reasonably be questioned.

(c) **Taking Notice.** The court:

   (1) may take judicial notice on its own; or

(2) must take judicial notice if a party requests it and the court is supplied with the necessary information.

(d)   Timing. The court may take judicial notice at any stage of the proceeding.

(e) Opportunity to Be Heard. On timely request, a party is entitled to be heard on the propriety of taking judicial notice and the nature of the fact to be noticed. If the court takes judicial notice before notifying a party, the party, on request, is still entitled to be heard.

(f)   Instructing the Jury. In a civil case, the court must instruct the jury to accept the noticed fact as conclusive. In a criminal case, the court must instruct the jury that it may or may not accept the noticed fact as conclusive.

2011 Advisory Committee Note. – The language of this rule has been amended as part of the restyling of the Evidence Rules to make them more easily understood and to make style and terminology consistent throughout the rules. These changes are intended to be stylistic only. There is no intent to change any result in any ruling on evidence admissibility. This rule is the federal rule, verbatim.

ADVISORY COMMITTEE NOTE

This rule is the federal rule, verbatim, and consolidates the law of judicial notice formerly contained in Rules 9 through 12, Utah Rules of Evidence (1971) and in Utah Code Annotated, § 78-25-1 (1953) into one broadly defined rule. The Utah Supreme Court has stated the rule with reference to judicial notice in Little Cottonwood Water Co. v. Kimball, 76 Utah 243, 267, 289 Pac. 116 (1930) where the court stated: "In short, a court is presumed to know what every man of ordinary intelligence must know about such things." See also DeFusion Co. v. Utah Liquor Control Comm'n, 613 P.2d 1120 (Utah 1980).

Subdivision (a) "governs only judicial notice of adjudicative facts," and does not deal with instances in which a court may notice legislative facts, which is left to the sound discretion of trial and appellate courts. Compare Rule 12, Utah Rules of Evidence (1971). Since legislative facts are matters that go to the policy of a rule of law as distinct from the true facts that are used in the adjudication of a controversy they are not appropriate for a rule of evidence and best left to the law-making considerations by appellate and trial courts.

Subdivision (b) is in accord with the Little Cottonwood Water Co. case, supra, and the substance of Rule 9(1) and (2), Utah Rules of Evidence (1971). Utah law presumes that the law of another jurisdiction is the same as that of the State of Utah and judicial notice has been taken from the law of other states and foreign countries. Lamberthv. Lamberth, 550 P.2d 200 (Utah 1976); Maple v. Maple, 566 P.2d 1229 (Utah 1977). The Utah court has taken judicial notice under Rule 9(2), Utah Rules of Evidence (1971) of the rules and regulations of the Tax Commission. Nelson v. State Tax Comm'n, 29 Utah 2d 162, 506 P.2d 437 (1973). The broad language of subdivision (b) is identical to Rule 201 of the Uniform Rules of Evidence (1974). Judicial notice of foreign law is permissible under this rule. Provisions of this rule supersede Utah Code Annotated, Section 78-25-1 (1953), since the statute is merely illustrative of items encompassed within the broad framework of this rule. The foreign law of some jurisdictions might best be left to proof through witnesses if the resort to sources available in the State of Utah is questionable.

Subdivision (c) is discretionary, but subdivision (d) requires the court to take judicial notice if requested by a party and if supplied with the necessary information to make a determination of whether to take judicial notice. Compare Rules 9(2) and 10(3), Utah Rules of Evidence (1971). The committee believes that Rule 201(d) simplifies the process of taking judicial notice of adjudicative facts by making it mandatory when a party makes a request therefor and supplies the court with the necessary information.

Subdivision (e) is similar to Rule 10(1), (2) and (3), Utah Rules of Evidence (1971).

Subdivision (g) is in accord with Rule 11, Utah Rules of Evidence (1971). The provision that in a criminal case the court shall instruct the jury that it may but is not required to accept as conclusive any fact judicially noticed has no counterpart in Utah Rules of Evidence (1971). Accord, State v. Lawrence, 120 Utah 323, 234 P.2d 600 (1951). See also Amendment VI, Constitution of the United States.

Article III Presumptions

Rule 301. Presumptions in Civil Cases Generally

In a civil case,

(a) unless a statute or these rules provide otherwise, the party against whom a presumption is directed has the burden of proving that the nonexistence of the presumed fact is more probable than its existence.

(b) If presumptions are inconsistent, the court determines which presumption applies based upon the weightier considerations of policy. If considerations of policy are of equal weight neither presumption applies.

2011 Advisory Committee Note. – The language of this rule has been amended as part of the restyling of the Evidence Rules to make them more easily understood and to make style and terminology consistent throughout the rules. These changes are intended to be stylistic only. There is no intent to change any result in any ruling on evidence admissibility.

ADVISORY COMMITTEE NOTE

The text of this rule is adapted from Rule 301, Wyoming Rules of Evidence (1977), which is Rule 301, Uniform Rules of Evidence (1974) except that the word "civil" is added in subdivision (a). Rule 301, Federal Rules of Evidence, is a substantially different rule than that promulgated by the United States Supreme Court. Rule 301, as originally proposed by the United States Supreme Court, placed the burden upon the opposing party of establishing the non-existence of a presumed fact once the party invoking the presumption had established sufficient facts to give rise to the presumption, but Rule 301 as promulgated by Congress adopted a substantially different rule limiting the effect of presumption, not otherwise controlled by statute, to one of going forward with proof rather than casting the burden of proof upon the opposing party.

Rule 14, Utah Rules of Evidence (1971) provided that except for presumptions which are conclusive or irrefutable, once the basic fact supporting the presumption is established "the presumption continues to exist and the burden of establishing the non-existence of the presumed fact is upon the party against whom the presumption operates . . . ." To the same effect, see Koesling v. Basamakis, 539 P.2d 1043 (Utah 1975). If evidence to rebut a presumption has not been admitted, the presumption will determine outcome on the issue; if such evidence has been admitted, the presumption will dictate the instruction to be given the jury on how they are to resolve doubt. There will continue to be fact combinations which satisfy the burden of going forward with the evidence but which are not "presumptions" within the meaning of this rule and which therefore do not shift the burden of persuasion. They might best be called "permissible inferences."

The Utah Rules of Evidence (1971) did not prohibit the application of presumptions in criminal cases. Presumptions in criminal cases are not treated in this rule. See Utah Code Annotated, Section 76-1-503 (1953) or any subsequent revision of that section. Recent decisions of the United States Supreme Court in Mullaney v. Wilbur, 421 U.S. 684 (1975) and Patterson v. New York, 432 U.S. 197 (1977) have given a constitutional dimension to presumptions in criminal cases.

Subdivision (b) is comparable in substance to Rule 15, Utah Rules of Evidence (1971). Utah law is believed to generally follow the position taken by the Uniform Rules of Evidence (1974) and the provisions of Article III as originally promulgated by the United States Supreme Court. See Presumptions in Utah: A Search for Certainty, 5 Utah L. Rev. 196 (1956).

Rule 302. Applying Federal Law to Presumptions in Civil Cases

In a civil case, federal law governs the effect of a presumption regarding a claim or defense for which federal law supplies the rule of decision.

2011 Advisory Committee Note. – The language of this rule has been amended as part of the restyling of the Evidence Rules to make them more easily understood and to make style and terminology consistent throughout the

rules. These changes are intended to be stylistic only. There is no intent to change any result in any ruling on evidence admissibility.

ADVISORY COMMITTEE NOTE

The text of this rule is taken from Rule 302, Uniform Rules of Evidence (1974). Presumptions in criminal cases are not treated in this rule. See Utah Code Annotated, Section 76-1-503 (1953) or any subsequent revision of that section.

Article IV Relevancy And Its Limits

Rule 401. Test for Relevant Evidence

Evidence is relevant if:

(a) it has any tendency to make a fact more or less probable than it would be without the evidence; and

(b) the fact is of consequence in determining the action.

2011 Advisory Committee Note. – The language of this rule has been amended as part of the restyling of the Evidence Rules to make them more easily understood and to make style and terminology consistent throughout the rules. These changes are intended to be stylistic only. There is no intent to change any result in any ruling on evidence admissibility. This rule is the federal rule, verbatim.

ADVISORY COMMITTEE NOTE

This rule is the federal rule, verbatim, and is comparable in substance to Rule 1(2), Utah Rules of Evidence (1971), but the former rule defined relevant evidence as that having a tendency to prove or disprove the existence of any "material fact." Avoiding the use of the term "material fact" accords with the application given to former Rule 1(2) by the Utah Supreme Court. State v. Peterson, 560 P.2d 1387 (Utah 1977).

Rule 402. General Admissibility of Relevant Evidence

Relevant evidence is admissible unless any of the following provides otherwise:

- the United States Constitution;
- the Utah Constitution;
- a statute; or
- rules applicable in courts of this state.

Irrelevant evidence is not admissible.

2011 Advisory Committee Note. – The language of this rule has been amended as part of the restyling of the Evidence Rules to make them more easily understood and to make style and terminology consistent throughout the rules. These changes are intended to be stylistic only. There is no intent to change any result in any ruling on evidence admissibility.

ADVISORY COMMITTEE NOTE

The text of this rule is Rule 402, Uniform Rules of Evidence (1974) except that prior to the word "statute" the words "Constitution of the United States" have been added.

Rule 403.   Excluding Relevant Evidence for Prejudice, Confusion, Waste of Time, or Other Reasons

The court may exclude relevant evidence if its probative value is substantially outweighed by a danger of one or more of the following: unfair prejudice, confusing the issues, misleading the jury, undue delay, wasting time, or needlessly presenting cumulative evidence.

2011 Advisory Committee Note. – The language of this rule has been amended as part of the restyling of the Evidence Rules to make them more easily understood and to make style and terminology consistent throughout the rules. These changes are intended to be stylistic only. There is no intent to change any result in any ruling on evidence admissibility. This rule is the federal rule, verbatim.

ADVISORY COMMITTEE NOTE

This rule is the federal rule, verbatim, and is substantively comparable to Rule 45, Utah Rules of Evidence (1971) except that "surprise" is not included as a basis for exclusion of relevant evidence. The change in language is not one of substance, since "surprise" would be within the concept of "unfair prejudice" as contained in Rule 403. See also Advisory Committee Note to Federal Rule 403 indicating that a continuance in most instances would be a more appropriate method of dealing with "surprise." See also Smith v. Estelle, 445 F. Supp. 647 (N.D. Tex. 1977)(surprise use of psychiatric testimony in capital case ruled prejudicial and violation of due process). See the following Utah cases to the same effect. Terry v. Zions Coop. Mercantile Inst., 605 P.2d 314 (Utah 1979); State v. Johns, 615 P.2d 1260 (Utah 1980); Reiser v. Lohner, 641 P.2d 93 (Utah 1982).

Rule 404. Character Evidence; Crimes or Other Acts

(a) **Character Evidence.**

(1) **Prohibited Uses.** Evidence of a person's character or character trait is not admissible to prove that on a particular occasion the person acted in conformity with the character or trait.

(2) Exceptions for a Defendant or Victim in a Criminal Case. The following exceptions apply in a criminal case:

    (A) a defendant may offer evidence of the defendant's pertinent trait, and if the evidence is admitted, the prosecutor may offer evidence to rebut it;

    (B) subject to the limitations in Rule 412, a defendant may offer evidence of an alleged victim's pertinent trait, and if the evidence is admitted, the prosecutor may:

        (i) offer evidence to rebut it; and

        (ii) offer evidence of the defendant's same trait; and

    (C) in a homicide case, the prosecutor may offer evidence of the alleged victim's trait of peacefulness to rebut evidence that the victim was the first aggressor.

(3) Exceptions for a Witness. Evidence of a witness's character may be admitted under Rules 607, 608, and 609.

(b) Crimes, Wrongs, or Other Acts.

    (1) Prohibited Uses. Evidence of a crime, wrong, or other act is not admissible to prove a person's character in order to show that on a particular occasion the person acted in conformity with the character.

    (2) Permitted Uses; Notice in a Criminal Case. This evidence may be admissible for another purpose, such as proving motive, opportunity, intent, preparation, plan, knowledge, identity, absence of mistake, or lack of accident. On request by a defendant in a criminal case, the prosecutor must:

(A) provide reasonable notice of the general nature of any such evidence that the prosecutor intends to offer at trial; and

(B) do so before trial, or during trial if the court excuses lack of pretrial notice on good cause shown.

(c) Evidence of Similar Crimes in Child-Molestation Cases.

(1) **Permitted Uses.** In a criminal case in which a defendant is accused of child molestation, the court may admit evidence that the defendant committed any other acts of child molestation to prove a propensity to commit the crime charged.

(2) **Disclosure.** If the prosecution intends to offer this evidence it shall provide reasonable notice in advance of trial, or during trial if the court excuses pretrial notice on good cause shown.

(3) For purposes of this rule "child molestation" means an act committed in relation to a child under the age of 14 which would, if committed in this state, be a sexual offense or an attempt to commit a sexual offense.

(4) Rule 404(c) does not limit the admissibility of evidence otherwise admissible under Rule 404(a), 404(b), or any other rule of evidence.

2011 Advisory Committee Note. – The language of this rule has been amended as part of the restyling of the Evidence Rules to make them more easily understood and to make style and terminology consistent throughout the rules. These changes are intended to be stylistic only. There is no intent to change any result in any ruling on evidence admissibility.

ADVISORY COMMITTEE NOTE.

Rule 404(a)-(b) is now Federal Rule of Evidence 404 verbatim. The 2001 amendments add the notice provisions already in the federal rule, add the amendments made to the federal rule effective December 1, 2000, and delete language added to the Utah Rule 404(b) in 1998. However, the deletion of that language is not intended to reinstate the holding of State v. Doporto, 935 P.2d 484 (Utah 1997). Evidence sought to be admitted under Rule 404(b) must also conform with Rules 402 and 403 to be admissible.

The 2008 amendment adds Rule 404(c). It applies in criminal cases where the accused is charged with a sexual offense against a child under the age of 14. Before evidence may be admitted under Rule 404(c), the trial court should conduct a hearing out of the presence of the jury to determine: (1) whether the accused committed other acts, which if committed in this State would constitute a sexual offense or an attempt to commit a sexual offense; (2) whether the evidence of other acts tends to prove the accused's propensity to commit the crime charged; and (3) whether under Rule 403 the danger of unfair prejudice substantially outweighs the probative value of the evidence, or whether for other reasons listed in Rule 403 the evidence should not be admitted. The court should consider the factors applicable as set forth in State v. Shickles, 760 P.2d 291, 295-96 (Utah 1988), which also may be applicable in determinations under Rule 404(b).

Upon the request of a party, the court may be required to provide a limiting instruction for evidence admitted under Rule 404(b) or (c).

Rule 405. Methods of Proving Character

(a) **By Reputation or Opinion.** When evidence of a person's character or character trait is admissible, it may be proved by testimony about the person's reputation or by testimony in the form of an opinion. On cross-examination of the character witness, the court may allow an inquiry into relevant specific instances of the person's conduct.

(b) **By Specific Instances of Conduct.** When a person's character or character trait is an essential element of a charge, claim, or defense, the character or trait may also be proved by relevant specific instances of the person's conduct.

2011 Advisory Committee Note. – The language of this rule has been amended as part of the restyling of the Evidence Rules to make them more easily understood and to make style and terminology consistent throughout the

rules. These changes are intended to be stylistic only. There is no intent to change any result in any ruling on evidence admissibility. This rule is the federal rule, verbatim.

ADVISORY COMMITTEE NOTE

This rule is the federal rule, verbatim, and is consistent with Rule 46, Utah Rules of Evidence (1971) and the decisions of the Utah Supreme Court. Cf. State v. Howard, 544 P.2d 466 (Utah 1975). Rule 47, Utah Rules of Evidence (1971) appears to be covered by subdivisions (a)(1) or (b) of Rule 404.

Rule 406. Habit; Routine Practice

Evidence of a person's habit or an organization's routine practice may be admitted to prove that on a particular occasion the person or organization acted in accordance with the habit or routine practice. The court may admit this evidence regardless of whether it is corroborated or whether there was an eyewitness.

2011 Advisory Committee Note. – The language of this rule has been amended as part of the restyling of the Evidence Rules to make them more easily understood and to make style and terminology consistent throughout the rules. These changes are intended to be stylistic only. There is no intent to change any result in any ruling on evidence admissibility. This rule is the federal rule, verbatim.

ADVISORY COMMITTEE NOTE

This rule is the federal rule, verbatim, and is comparable to Rule 49, Utah Rules of Evidence (1971). The substance of Rule 50, Utah Rules of Evidence (1971) providing for the method of proof of habit or custom and allowing evidence in the form of opinion as well as specific instances when the number of instances is sufficient to warrant a finding of habit or custom was deleted by Congress with a note by the House Judiciary Committee that the method of proof should be left with the Court. Compare Rule 406(b), Uniform Rules of Evidence (1974), which is Rule 406(b) as originally promulgated by the United States Supreme Court.

Rule 407. Subsequent Remedial Measures

When measures are taken that would have made an earlier event that caused injury or harm less likely to occur, evidence of the subsequent measures is not admissible to prove:

- negligence;
- culpable conduct;
- a defect in a product or its design; or
- a need for a warning or instruction.

But the court may admit this evidence for another purpose, such as impeachment or — if disputed — proving ownership, control, or the feasibility of precautionary measures.

2011 Advisory Committee Note. – The language of this rule has been amended as part of the restyling of the Evidence Rules to make them more easily understood and to make style and terminology consistent throughout the rules. These changes are intended to be stylistic only. There is no intent to change any result in any ruling on evidence admissibility.

ADVISORY COMMITTEE NOTE

These amendments conform to amendments made to the Federal Rule in 1997, and the rule is now the Federal Rule, verbatim.

Notes of Federal Advisory Committee on Rules - 1997 Amendment

The amendment to Rule 407 makes two changes in the rule. First, the words "an injury or harm allegedly caused by" were added to clarify that the rule applies only to changes made after the occurrence that produced the damages giving rise to the action. Evidence of measures taken by the defendant prior to the "event" causing "injury or harm" do not fall within the exclusionary scope of Rule 407 even if they occurred after the manufacture or design of the product. See Chase v. General Motors Corp., 856 F.2d 17, 21-22 (4th Cir. 1988).

Second, Rule 407 has been amended to provide that evidence of subsequent remedial measures may not be used to prove "a defect in a product or its design, or that a warning or instruction should have accompanied a product." This amendment adopts the view of a majority of the circuits that have interpreted Rule 407 to apply to products liability actions. See Raymond v. Raymond Corp., 938 F.2d 1518, 1522 (1st Cir. 1991); In re Joint Eastern District and Southern District Asbestos Litigation v. Armstrong World Industries, Inc., 995 F.2d 343 (2d Cir. 1993); Cann v. Ford Motor Co., 658 F.2d 54, 60 (2d Cir. 1981), cert. denied, 456 U.S. 960 (1982); Kelly v. Crown Equipment Co., 970 F.2d 1273, 1275 (3d Cir. 1992); Werner v. Upjohn, Inc., 628 F.2d 848 (4th Cir. 1980), cert. denied, 449 U.S. 1080 (1981); Grenada Steel Industries, Inc. v. Alabama Oxygen Co., Inc., 695 F.2d 883 (5th Cir. 1983); Bauman v. Volkswagenwerk Aktiengesellschaft, 621 F.2d 230, 232 (6th Cir. 1980); Flaminio v. Honda Motor Company, Ltd., 733 F.2d 463, 469 (7th Cir. 1984); Gauthier v. AMF, Inc., 788 F.2d 634, 636-37 (9th Cir. 1986).

Although this amendment adopts a uniform federal rule, it should be noted that evidence of subsequent remedial measures may be admissible pursuant to the second sentence of Rule 407. Evidence of subsequent measures that is not barred by Rule 407 may still be subject to exclusion on Rule 403 grounds when the dangers of prejudice or confusion substantially outweigh the probative value of the evidence.

GAP Report on Rule 407.

The words "injury or harm" were substituted for the word "event" in line 3. The stylization changes in the second sentence of the rule were eliminated. The words "causing 'injury or harm' " were added to the Committee Note.

Rule 408.   Compromise Offers and Negotiations

(a) Prohibited Uses. Evidence of the following is not admissible either to prove or disprove liability for or the validity or amount of a disputed claim:

(1) furnishing, promising, or offering — or accepting, promising to accept, or offering to accept — a valuable consideration in order to compromise or attempt to compromise the claim; and

(2) conduct or a statement made in compromise negotiations.

(b) Exceptions.

(1) The court may admit this evidence for another purpose, such as proving a witness's bias or prejudice, negating a contention of undue delay, or proving an effort to obstruct a criminal investigation or prosecution.

(2) The court is not required to exclude evidence otherwise discoverable merely because it is presented in the course of compromise negotiations.

2011 Advisory Committee Note. – The language of this rule has been amended as part of the restyling of the Evidence Rules to make them more easily understood and to make style and terminology consistent throughout the rules. These changes are intended to be stylistic only. There is no intent to change any result in any ruling on evidence admissibility.

ADVISORY COMMITTEE NOTE

This rule is the federal rule, verbatim, and is comparable to Rules 52 and 53, Utah Rules of Evidence (1971) but is broader to the extent that it excludes statements made in the course of negotiations.

Rule 409. Payment of medical and similar expenses; expressions of apology

(a) Evidence of furnishing, promising to pay, or offering to pay medical, hospital, or similar expenses resulting from an injury is not admissible to prove liability for the injury.

(b) Evidence of unsworn statements, affirmations, gestures, or conduct made to a patient or a person associated with the patient by a defendant that expresses the following is not admissible in a malpractice action against a health care provider or an employee of a health care provider to prove liability for an injury;

    (1) apology, sympathy, commiseration, condolence, compassion, or general sense of benevolence; or

    (2) a description of the sequence of events relating to the unanticipated outcome of medical care or the significance of events.

2011 Advisory Committee Note. – The language of section (a) of this rule has been amended as part of the restyling of the Evidence Rules to make them more easily understood and to make style and terminology consistent throughout the rules. These changes are intended to be stylistic only. There is no intent to change any result in any ruling on evidence admissibility.

The language of section (b), promulgated by the Utah Legislature in 2011 (HJR 38), is unchanged.

ADVISORY COMMITTEE NOTE

There was no comparable rule under Utah Rules of Evidence (1971) but former Rules 52 and 53 seemed to encompass the same restrictions. Utah Code Annotated, Sections 78-27-29, 78-27-30 and 31-1-15 (1953) are superseded by this rule.

LEGISLATIVE NOTE

In 2010 the Utah Legislature amended Rule 409 by a two-thirds vote in both houses adding paragraph (b) and making related changes. In 2011 the Legislature further amended the rule by a two-thirds vote in both houses to make it follow more closely Utah Code Ann. Sec. 78B-3-422.

The intent and purpose of amending the rule with paragraph (b) is to encourage expressions of apology, empathy, and condolence and the disclosure of facts and circumstances related to unanticipated outcomes in the provision of health care in an effort to facilitate the timely and satisfactory resolution of patient concerns arising from unanticipated outcomes in the provision of health care. Patient records are not statements made to patients, and therefore are not inadmissible under this rule.

Effective date. House Joint Resolution 38 takes effect upon approval by a constitutional two-thirds vote of all members elected to each house. [March 8, 2011]

Rule 410. Pleas, Plea Discussions, and Related Statements

(a) Prohibited Uses. In a civil or criminal case, evidence of the following is not admissible against the defendant who made the plea or participated in the plea discussions:

  (1) a guilty plea that was later withdrawn;

  (2) a nolo contendere plea;

  (3) a statement made during a proceeding on either of those pleas under Federal Rule of Criminal Procedure 11 or a comparable state procedure; or

  (4) a statement made during plea discussions with an attorney for the prosecuting authority if the discussions did not result in a guilty plea or they resulted in a later-withdrawn guilty plea.

(b) Exceptions. The court may admit a statement described in Rule 410(a)(3) or (4):

(1) in any proceeding in which another statement made during the same plea or plea discussions has been introduced, if in fairness the statements ought to be considered together; or

(2) in a criminal proceeding for perjury or false statement, if the defendant made the statement under oath, on the record, and with counsel present.

2011 Advisory Committee Note. – The language of this rule has been amended as part of the restyling of the Evidence Rules to make them more easily understood and to make style and terminology consistent throughout the rules. These changes are intended to be stylistic only. There is no intent to change any result in any ruling on evidence admissibility. This rule is the federal rule, verbatim.

ADVISORY COMMITTEE NOTE

This rule is the federal rule, verbatim. There was no comparable rule in the Utah Rules of Evidence (1971). However, withdrawn pleas of guilty have been ruled inadmissible by the Utah Supreme Court. State v. Jensen, 74 Utah 299, 279 P. 506 (1929).

Rule 410(4) does not cover plea negotiations with public officials other than prosecuting attorneys. There are still constitutional limitations on the use of statements obtained from suspects. See Miranda v. Arizona, 384 U.S. 436, 86 S. Ct. 1602, 16 L. Ed. 2d 694 (1966); Massiah v. United States, 377 U.S. 201, 84 S. Ct. 1199, 12 L. Ed. 2d 246 (1964).

Rule 411. Liability Insurance

Evidence that a person was or was not insured against liability is not admissible to prove whether the person acted negligently or otherwise wrongfully. But the court may admit this evidence for another purpose, such as proving a witness's bias or prejudice or proving agency, ownership, or control.

2011 Advisory Committee Note. – The language of this rule has been amended as part of the restyling of the Evidence Rules to make them more easily understood and to make style and terminology consistent throughout the rules. These changes are intended to be stylistic only. There is no intent to change any result in any ruling on evidence admissibility. This rule is the federal rule, verbatim.

ADVISORY COMMITTEE NOTE

This rule is the federal rule, verbatim. The provisions of this rule are comparable to Rule 54, Utah Rules of Evidence (1971) and case law. Cf. Robinson v. Hreinson, 17 Utah 2d 261, 409 P.2d 121 (1965); Reid v. Owens, 98 Utah 50, 93 P.2d 680 (1939).

Rule 412. Admissibility of Victim's Sexual Behavior or Predisposition

(a) **Prohibited Uses.** The following evidence is not admissible in a criminal proceeding involving alleged sexual misconduct:

(1) evidence offered to prove that a victim engaged in other sexual behavior; or

(2) evidence offered to prove a victim's sexual predisposition.

(b) **Exceptions.** The court may admit the following evidence if the evidence is otherwise admissible under these rules:

(1) evidence of specific instances of a victim's sexual behavior, if offered to prove that someone other than the defendant was the source of semen, injury, or other physical evidence;

(2) evidence of specific instances of a victim's

sexual behavior with respect to the person accused of the sexual misconduct, if offered by the defendant to prove consent or if offered by the prosecutor; or

(3) evidence whose exclusion would violate the defendant's constitutional rights.

(c) Procedure to Determine Admissibility.

(1) Motion. If a party intends to offer evidence under Rule 412(b), the party must:

(A) file a motion that specifically describes the evidence and states the purpose for which it is to be offered;

(B) do so at least 14 days before trial unless the court, for good cause, sets a different time; and

(C) serve the motion on all parties.

(2) Notice to the Victim. The prosecutor shall timely notify the victim

or, when appropriate, the victim's guardian or representative.

(3) Hearing. Before admitting evidence under this rule, the court must conduct an in camera hearing and give the victim and parties a right to attend and be heard. Unless the court orders otherwise, the motion, related materials, and the record of the hearing are classified as protected.

(d) Definition of "Victim." In this rule, "victim" includes an alleged victim.

2016 Advisory Committee Note. The 2016 amendment changes the classification of records described in subparagraph (c)(3) from sealed to protected. See CJA Rule 4-202.02.

Effective May 1, 2017

Rule 416. Violation of Traffic Code Not Admissible.

Evidence that a person was convicted of an infraction or a class C misdemeanor under Utah Code Annotated Title 41, Chapter 6a, is not admissible:

(a) to prove the person acted negligently or otherwise wrongly, or

(b) to impeach the person's testimony on those issues.

2011 Advisory Committee Note. – The language of this rule has been amended as part of the restyling of the Evidence Rules to make them more easily understood and to make style and terminology consistent throughout the rules. These changes are intended to be stylistic only. There is no intent to change any result in any ruling on evidence admissibility.

ADVISORY COMMITTEE NOTE.

Rule numbers 413, 414 and 415 are reserved.

Article V Privileges

Rule 501. Privilege in General

A claim of privilege to withhold evidence is governed by:

(a)   The Constitution of the United States;

(b)   The Constitution of the State of Utah;

(c)   These rules of evidence;

(d)   Other rules adopted by the Utah Supreme Court;

(e)   Decisions of the Utah courts; and

(f)   Existing statutory provisions not in conflict with the above.

2011 Advisory Committee Note. – The language of this rule has been amended as part of the restyling of the Evidence Rules to make them more easily understood and to make style and terminology consistent throughout the rules. These changes are intended to be stylistic only. There is no intent to change any result in any ruling on evidence admissibility.

ADVISORY COMMITTEE NOTE

It is in the nature of evidentiary privileges that they interfere with establishment of the whole truth. As a consequence, some members of the Committee thought that all statutory privileges not important enough to be incorporated in Article V should be expressly invalidated. Most members, however, felt that in spite of the truth-impeding effect of privileges, the already-existing legislatively created privileges should be preserved. Members of the majority expressed various views:

(1) Privileges reflect good policy choices, fostering candor in important relationships by promising protection of confidential disclosures.

(2) Even if the statutory privileges are not all wise, the legislature has by democratic process resolved policy disputes and should not be lightly overturned. Under the Utah Constitution, art. VIII, § 4, while the Supreme Court has the basic power to establish rules of privilege, the legislature also has a role, since it is empowered to make amendments by a two-thirds vote of all members of both houses of the legislature. Even the Committee members who would abolish statutory privileges recognized the dismaying magnitude of the task of reevaluating every existing privilege separately.

(3) The statutory privileges most often invoked are the traditional ones dealt with in other sections of Article V. The other statutory privileges are relied on rarely, if at all, so that their perpetuation will have almost no impact on court proceedings. If problems involving these more exotic privileges do arise, that is the time for the Court to deal with them.

Rule 501 acknowledges the existence of other privileges created by federal and state constitutions, such as the exclusion of the fruits of unreasonable searches and seizures, of coerced confessions, and of compulsory self-incrimination.

Rule 501 also accepts all pre-existing statutory privileges, except those inconsistent with these rules. In particular, Utah Code Ann. § 78-24-8, insofar as it defines privileges relating to spouses, attorneys, clergy, and physicians, § 58-25a-8, with respect to psychologists, and § 58-35-10, with respect to social workers, are made ineffectual by the adoption of rules specifically redefining those privileges.

The Supreme Court has the power to create rules of privilege formally. It can also create or reshape privileges by its decisions in concrete cases. However, the language of 501, that there are no non-rule, non-statutory privileges, serves as a declaration by the Court that it intends to operate normally through formal rule-making procedures.

The Committee made an effort to identify all the statutes in effect in 1989 that specifically provided for a privilege. Other than privileges dealt with in other rules, they are listed below. Statutes that merely imply the existence of a privilege are also included, marked by asterisks. Even though the Committee's own search was augmented by Judge Michael L. Hutchings' article "Privileges in Utah Law," Utah Bar Journal 2:3:34 (Mar. 1989), there may be still other such provisions.

Witnesses.

§ 78-24-9 (witness need not answer degrading question unless it is closely related to a fact in issue or is conviction of a felony);

Grand jury.

§ 77-10a-13 (grand juror may not disclose how any juror voted, though grand juror can be compelled to disclose what jurors said);

Interpreter.

§ 78-24a-10 (information communicated through an interpreter for the hearing-impaired that is otherwise privileged);

Health care data.

§ 26-3-9 (health care data collected by Department of Health);

§§ 26-25a-101 and -102 (communicable disease data collected by health departments) (cf. § 26-6-20.5);

§ 26-25-3 (medical information gathered for medical research);

§ 76-7-313 (information on abortions);

§ 31A-22-617(4)(c) (health care data audited by Department of Health);

§§ 26-6a-6* and -7* (test for AIDS);

§ 58-17-16* (pharmacy may not release patient's medical profile except to drug law enforcement or at patient's direction; the implication is that it may not be obtained in civil litigation);

Professionals working with social or psychological problems.

§ 58-41-16 (speech pathologist);

§ 30-1-37 (marriage counselor);

§ 58-39-10 (marriage counselor);

§ 30-3-17.1* (communications to court-appointed domestic relations counselors working toward marital reconciliation; subject to "public interests" under § 78-24-8(5));

§ 78-24-8 (sexual assault counselor);

§ 78-3c-4 (sexual assault counselor);

§ 53A-24-107 (individual information of persons being rehabilitated, except in enforcement of law);

Results of private investigations.

§ 58-12-43(7) (information collected by professional committee investigating a doctor);

§ 78-14-15 (evidence presented to medical malpractice panel);

§ 34-38-13 (results of employer tests for drugs or alcohol);

§ 78-27-49 (no private financial information obtained from a bank without court order "shall be admissible");

Government information.

§ 78-24-8 (communications to public officers in official confidence);

§ 35-9-14* (trade secrets communicated to Industrial Commission can be used only in enforcement of Occupational Safety and Health Act and then under protective order);

§ 78-7-30(3)* (information in proceedings before Judicial Conduct Commission "are privileged in any civil action," except where subpoenaed in case challenging judicial conduct as improper or except when judge does not resign within 6 months);

§ 76-8-708 (college administrator "cannot be examined" as to information obtained by procedures for enforcing school rules);

§§ 63-2-201 and 63-2-202* (confidential information in state archives);

§ 41-2-201* (information provided by doctor or expert in physical, mental or emotional disabilities in determining whether to issue a restricted driver's license to an "impaired" person is "confidential");

§ 41-6-40 (compulsory automobile accident reports);

§ 54-4-16 (accident reports filed by public utility with Public Service Commission);

§ 41-6-170 (traffic convictions);

§ 77-18-2(4) and (5)(records of expungement of conviction);

§ 77-27-21.5(12)* (sex offender registration);

§ 77-18-1(4) (presentence report);

§ 78-24-10 (compelled testimony about fraudulent conveyances);

§ 63-53a-6 (information collected by governor concerning state energy resources);

§ 73-22-6* (logs of geothermal wells);

§ 40-8-8* (confidential information communicated to Board of Oil, Gas and Mining "shall be protected and not become public records" unless waived or mining operation terminates);

§ 7-1-802* (reports to Commissioner of Financial Institutions);

§ 70C-8-103(5)* (identity of persons investigated by Department of Financial Institutions but not subject of enforcement proceedings);

§ 13-11-7(2)* (identity of persons investigated for consumer sales fraud but not subject to enforcement proceedings).

In addition to statutes which directly or indirectly create evidentiary privileges, there are a great many statutes which seem to impose a professional or institutional obligation of keeping confidence, yet do not clearly exempt the information from subpoena. A great many of the provisions cited by Hutchings are of this sort. A few examples are:

§ 78-3e-2 (identity of persons informing about drugs in schools, "shall be kept confidential");

§ 26-4-17 (autopsy report is "confidential," though it can be released to police, relatives, or attending physician);

§ 65A-1-10 (proprietary geologic or financial information communicated to Division of State Lands and Forestry; the board "may" keep it confidential).

Rule 502. Husband - Wife

(a)   Definition.

(1) "Confidential communication" means a communication:

    (A) made privately by any person to his or her spouse; and

    (B) not intended for disclosure to any other person.

(b)   Privilege in Criminal Proceedings. In a criminal proceeding, a wife may not be compelled to testify against her husband, nor a husband against his wife.

(c)   Statement of the Privilege. An individual has a privilege during the person's life:

(1) to refuse to testify or to prevent his or her spouse or former spouse from testifying as to any confidential communication made by the individual to the spouse during their marriage; and

(2) to prevent another person from disclosing any such confidential communication.

(d)   Who May Claim Privilege. The privilege may be claimed by:

(1) the person who made the confidential communication;

(2) the person's guardian or conservator;

(3) the non-communicating spouse to whom the confidential communication was made may claim the privilege on behalf of the person who made the confidential communication during the life of the communicating spouse.

(e)   Exceptions to the Privilege. No privilege exists under paragraph (c) in the following circumstances:

(1) Spouses as Adverse Parties. In a civil proceeding in which the spouses are adverse parties;

(2) Furtherance of Crime or Tort. As to any communication which was made, in whole or in part, to enable or aid anyone to commit; to plan to commit; or to conceal a crime or a tort.

(3) Spouse Charged with Crime or Tort. In a proceeding in which one spouse is charged with a crime or a tort against the person or property of:

    (A) the other spouse;

    (B) the child of either spouse;

    (C) a person residing in the household of either spouse; or

    (D) a third person if the crime or tort is committed in the course of committing a crime or tort against any of the persons named above.

(4) Interest of Minor Child. If the interest of a minor child of either spouse may be adversely affected, the Court may refuse to allow invocation of the privilege.

2011 Advisory Committee Note. – The language of this rule has been amended as part of the restyling of the Evidence Rules to make them more easily understood and to make style and terminology consistent throughout the rules. These changes are intended to be stylistic only. There is no intent to change any result in any ruling on evidence admissibility.

ADVISORY COMMITTEE NOTE

Evidentiary privilege concerning the marriage relationship has taken two basic forms. First, a testimonial privilege shields one spouse from testifying against the other. Second, a communications privilege prevents disclosure of confidential communications between spouses (sometimes expanded to information learned by virtue of the marriage relationship). Each form of the privilege is further defined by who can invoke the privilege, whether it extends to civil as well as criminal proceedings, and the exceptions to the privilege.

In Utah, both forms of the privilege are recognized. Article I, section 12 of the Utah Constitution provides that "a wife shall not be compelled to testify against her husband, nor a husband against his wife." See Utah Code Ann. § 77-1-6(2)(d) (1990) (same). Utah Code Ann. § 78-24-8(1) (Cum. Supp. 1991) provides:

(a) Neither a wife nor a husband may either during the marriage or afterwards be, without the consent of the other, examined as to any communication made by one to the other during the marriage.

(b) This exception does not apply:

(i) to a civil action or proceeding by one spouse against the other;

(ii) to a criminal action or proceeding for a crime committed by one spouse against the other;

(iii) to the crime of deserting or neglecting to support a spouse or child;

(iv) to any civil or criminal proceeding for abuse or neglect committed against the child of either spouse; or

(v) if otherwise specially provided by law.

As the Utah Supreme Court has noted in a case in which the husband was a criminal defendant, the Utah Constitution and the statute together give "both the husband and the wife a privilege that the wife shall not testify under these circumstances without the consent of both the husband and the wife." State v. Brown, 14 Utah 2d 324, 383 P.2d 930, 932 (1963). The Court recently declared in a criminal case that the scope of the testimonial privilege is an open issue when the non-testifying defendant spouse asserts it: "Whether Section 78-24-8(1) envisions an absolute privilege to prevent a spouse from testifying without the consent of the other, or whether that privilege pertains to communications only, is an issue we leave for another day." State v. Bundy, 684 P.2d 58, 61 (Utah 1986);

cf. State v. Wilson, 771 P.2d 1077 (Utah App. 1989). As for the communications privilege in the Utah statute, it is noteworthy that neither the statute nor the case law answers directly who is the holder of the communications privilege, although the statutory language suggests that both spouses hold the privilege for communications between them.

The Committee was convinced that Utah law on marital privilege needs clarification and reform. Both forms of marital privilege and the various features of the privilege - the holder, the scope, and exceptions - were addressed. In doing so, the Committee recognized that "[t]he need to develop all relevant facts is both fundamental and comprehensive." United States v. Nixon, 418 U.S. 683, 709 (1974). The Committee also considered competing values supporting the privilege. The traditional justifications for the testimonial privilege have been the prevention of marital dissension and the repugnance of requiring a person to condemn or be condemned by his or her spouse. 8 Wigmore §§ 2228, 2241 (McNaughton Rev. 1961). Although these justifications are important, the Committee concluded that they are insufficient to justify a spousal privilege covering non-communicative conduct. In short, the Committee recommended against adoption of a testimonial privilege that either spouse could invoke. Accordingly, the Committee recommended that any marital privilege be limited to confidential communications.

This position comports with the view of many leading commentators on evidence who oppose the testimonial privilege because it does not promote marital felicity, is based on the outmoded concept that the husband and wife are one, and causes suppression of relevant evidence. For example, Wigmore called the privilege "a legal anachronism." 8 Wigmore § 2228 at 221 (McNaughton Rev. 1961). However, for the Committee's full recommendation to be adopted, the following language from art. I, § 12 of the Utah Constitution would need to be repealed: "a wife shall not be compelled to testify against her husband, nor a husband against his wife."

The Committee's preferred rule would not include subparagraph (a) and would accordingly require constitutional change. Absent constitutional change, the rule repeats the state constitutional testimonial privilege for criminal cases in subparagraph (a), to be asserted or waived by the witness spouse. For all other circumstances in which the Rules of Evidence apply, including civil and criminal proceedings, the Committee proposed a privilege for confidential husband-wife communications. Subparagraph (b)(1) is patterned after Rule 504(a) of the Uniform Rules of Evidence (1974), and subparagraph (b)(2) is patterned after Rule 504(a) of the Uniform Rules of Evidence (1986). Although empirical validation is problematic, several on the Committee supported a communications privilege as needed to encourage marital confidences, which in turn promote marital harmony. More persuasive to the Committee was the interest in securing an expectation of privacy pertaining to confidential communications between spouses. This expectation interest is based in part on whatever reliance married couples have placed on their understanding of existing marital privilege law. It is based as well on the private nature of the marriage relationship. Judge Weinstein states the argument: "[T]he stresses of modern society make more attractive than ever before the prospect of safe harbor of intimacy where spouses can confide in each other freely without any fear that what they say will be published under compulsion." 2 J. Weinstein & M. Berger, Weinstein's Evidence p. 505[02] at 505-12 (1986).

The Committee decided that the communications privilege should apply in civil and criminal proceedings. Many Committee members thought that limiting the privilege to criminal proceedings would fail adequately to protect from intrusive civil process the interests secured by the privilege.

Subparagraph (b)(3) makes the communicating spouse the holder of the privilege, which is consistent with the policy of encouraging freedom of communication and follows the view of leading commentators. E.g., 8 Wigmore, Evidence § 2340(1) (McNaughton Rev. 1961); McCormick on Evidence § 83 at 198 (E. Cleary ed., 1984).

Under this view, in the case of a unilateral oral message or statement, of a husband to his wife, only the husband could assert the privilege, where the sole purpose is to show the expressions and attitude of the husband. If the object, however, were to show the wife's adoption of the husband's statement by her silence, then the husband's statement and her conduct both become her communication and she can claim the privilege. Similarly, if a conversation or an exchange of correspondence between them is offered to show the collective expressions of them both, either it seems could claim privilege as to the entire exchange.

Id. See also, Rule 28(1), Utah Rules of Evidence (1971). The Committee intends that, during the life of the communicating spouse, the non-communicating spouse may claim the privilege on behalf of the communicating spouse if the latter is alive but not present to assert it. Upon the death of the communicating spouse, the privilege ceases to exist.

The exceptions in subparagraph (b)(4) of the proposed rule represent circumstances, in the Committee's judgment, in which the values of encouraging marital confidences and protecting spousal expectation of privacy are at their weakest or simply cannot stand in the way of the production of evidence that is relevant to the ascertainment of significant legal rights. They are patterned upon Rule 504(c) of the Uniform Rules of Evidence (1986) and are similar to the exceptions contained in Utah Code Ann. § 78-24-8(1) (Cum. Supp. 1991) and Rules 23(2) and 28 of the Utah Rules of Evidence (1971). The exceptions apply only to subparagraph (b) because art. I, § 12 of the Utah Constitution prevents their application to subparagraph (a).

The person making the confidential communication is entitled not only to refuse to disclose the communication, but also to prevent disclosure by the present or former spouse or others who, without the knowledge of the person making the confidential communication, learn its content. Problems of waiver are dealt with in Rule 507.

The Committee felt that exceptions to the privilege should be specifically enumerated, and further endorsed the concept that in the area of exceptions, the rule should simply state that no privilege existed, rather than expressing the exception in terms of a "waiver" of the privilege. The Committee wanted to avoid any possible clashes with the common law concepts of "waiver."

Rule 503. Communications to Clergy.

(a)   Definitions.

> (1)   "Cleric" means a minister, priest, rabbi, or other similar functionary of a religious organization or an individual reasonably believed to be so by the person consulting that individual.

> (2)   "Confidential Communication" means a communication:

>> (A)   made privately; and

>> (B)   not intended for further disclosure except to other persons in furtherance of the purpose of the communication.

(b) Statement of the Privilege. A person has a privilege to refuse to disclose, and to prevent another from disclosing, any confidential communication:

> (1) made to a cleric in the cleric's religious capacity; and

> (2) necessary and proper to enable the cleric to discharge the function of the cleric's office according to the usual course of practice or discipline.

(c) Who May Claim the Privilege. The privilege may be claimed by:

> (1) the person who made the confidential communication;

> (2) the person's guardian or conservator;

> (3) the person's personal representative if the person is deceased; and

> (4) the person who was the cleric at the time of the communication on behalf of the communicant.

2011 Advisory Committee Note. – The language of this rule has been amended as part of the restyling of the Evidence Rules to make them more easily understood and to make style and terminology consistent throughout the rules. These changes are intended to be stylistic only. There is no intent to change any result in any ruling on evidence admissibility.

ADVISORY COMMITTEE NOTE

The considerations that support evidentiary privileges for confidential communications generally favor a privilege for confidential communications made to a member of the clergy, at least to the extent that the communication is entrusted to the cleric in the cleric's religious capacity. See 8 Wigmore, Evidence § 2396 at 878. See also Utah Code Ann. § 78-24-8(3).

The Committee chose the form of the proposed Rule 506 of the Federal Rules of Evidence (never adopted) for clarity and for consistency with the Committee's proposed Rule 502. See, e.g., 51 F.R.D. 315, 371-73. The Committee began with the basic concept of the current rule stated in Utah Code Ann. § 78-24-8(3), making changes as discussed below.

(a) Definitions. Subparagraph (1) defines the term "cleric" to include a "minister, priest, rabbi, or other similar functionary of a religious organization." The non-denominational and gender neutral term "cleric" replaces the terms "priest" and "clergyman" traditionally used in statements of the privilege, but embraces the same concept. Subparagraph (1) expands the scope of the concept, however, by including as a cleric "an individual reasonably believed so to be by the person consulting that individual."

Subparagraph (2) defines a confidential communication consistently with proposed Rule 502.

(b) General rule of privilege. The scope of the proposed privilege falls between a privilege narrowly restricted to doctrinally required confessions and a privilege broadly applicable to all confidential communications with a cleric. The privilege includes confessions, but also applies to all confidential communications to the cleric that are (1) "in the cleric's religious capacity" and (2) "necessary and proper for the cleric's office according to the usual course of practice or discipline." The privilege does not extend to confidential communications with a cleric when the cleric is acting in any capacity other than the religious capacity.

The term "in the cleric's religious capacity" was chosen over "in the cleric's professional character" to avoid an implication that only communications with professional members of the clergy are protected. The privilege applies to confidential communications with lay clerics as well.

The language "necessary and proper for the cleric to discharge the functions of the cleric's office according to the usual course of practice or discipline" replaces "in the course of discipline enjoined by the church to which he belongs" in order to extend the privilege beyond doctrinally required confessions. For similar language, see Iowa

Code Ann. 1950 Section 622.10. See also, State v. Burkett, 357 N.W.2d 632 (Iowa 1984) for an application of the Iowa statute.

(c) Who may claim the privilege. The person who makes the confidential communication holds the privilege, but the rule provides that others may claim the privilege for that person in certain circumstances. A cleric is presumed to have authority to claim the privilege for the communicant, though the presumption may be overcome by a preponderance of evidence to the contrary. See Rule of Evidence 301 (a).

Under the privilege as phrased, the person making the confidential communication is entitled not only to refuse to disclose the communication, but also to prevent the disclosure by the cleric or others who, by presence in furtherance of the religious purpose or by overhearing without the knowledge of the person making the communication, may know the content of the communication. Problems of waiver are dealt with by Rule 507.

The Committee felt that exceptions to the privilege should be specifically enumerated, and further endorsed the concept that in the area of exceptions, the rule should simply state that no privilege existed, rather than expressing the exception in terms of a "waiver" of the privilege. The Committee wanted to avoid any possible clashes with the common law concepts of "waiver."

Rule 504. Lawyer - Client.

(a) Definitions.

(1) "Client" means a person, public officer, corporation, association, or other organization or entity, either public or private, who is rendered professional legal services by a lawyer or who consults a lawyer with a view to obtaining professional legal services.

(2) "Lawyer" means a person authorized, or reasonably believed by the client to be authorized, to practice law in any state or nation.

(3) "Representative of the lawyer" means a person or entity employed to assist the lawyer in a rendition of professional legal services.

(4) "Representative of the client" means a person or entity having authority:

    (A) to obtain professional legal services;

    (B) to act on advice rendered pursuant to legal services on behalf of the client; or

    (C) person or entity specifically authorized to communicate with the lawyer concerning a legal matter.

(5) "Communication" includes:

    (A) advice given by the lawyer in the course of representing the client; and

    (B) disclosures of the client and the client's representatives to the lawyer or the lawyer's representatives incidental to the professional relationship.

(6) "Confidential communication" means a communication not intended to be disclosed to third persons other than those to whom disclosure is in furtherance of rendition of professional legal services to the client or those reasonably necessary for the transmission of the communication.

(b) Statement of the Privilege. A client has a privilege to refuse to disclose, and to prevent any other person from disclosing, confidential communications:

(1) made for the purpose of facilitating the rendition of professional legal services to the client; and

(2) the communications were between:

(A) the client and the client's representatives, lawyers, lawyer's representatives, and lawyers representing others in matters of common interest; or

(B) among the client's representatives, lawyers, lawyer's representatives, and lawyers representing others in matters of common interest.

(c) Who May Claim the Privilege. The privilege may be claimed by:

(1) the client;

(2) the client's guardian or conservator;

(3) the personal representative of a client who is deceased;

(4) the successor, trustee, or similar representative of a client that was a corporation, association, or other organization, whether or not in existence; and

(5) the lawyer on behalf of the client.

(d) Exceptions to the Privilege. Privilege does not apply in the following circumstances:

(1) Furtherance of the Crime or Fraud. If the services of the lawyer were sought or obtained to enable or aid anyone to commit or plan to commit what the client knew or reasonably should have known to be a crime or fraud;

(2) Claimants through Same Deceased Client. As to a communication relevant to an issue between parties who claim through the same deceased client, regardless of whether the claims are by testate or intestate succession or by inter vivos transaction;

(3) Breach of Duty by Lawyer or Client. As to a communication relevant to an issue of breach of duty by the lawyer to the client;

(4) Document Attested by Lawyer. As to a communication relevant to an issue concerning a document to which the lawyer was an attesting witness; or

(5) Joint Clients. As to the communication relevant to a matter of common interest between two or more clients if the communication was made by any of them to a lawyer retained or consulted in common, when offered in an action between any of the clients.

2011 Advisory Committee Note. – The language of this rule has been amended as part of the restyling of the Evidence Rules to make them more easily understood and to make style and terminology consistent throughout the rules. These changes are intended to be stylistic only. There is no intent to change any result in any ruling on evidence admissibility.

ADVISORY COMMITTEE NOTE

Rule 504 is based upon proposed Rule 503 of the United States Supreme Court. Rule 504 would replace and supersede Utah Code Ann. § 78-24-8(2) and is intended to be consistent with the ethical obligations of confidentiality set forth in Rule 1.6 of the Utah Rules of Professional Conduct.

The Committee revised the proposed rule of the United States Supreme Court to address the issues raised in Upjohn Co. v. United States, 449 U.S. 383, 101 S. Ct. 677 (1981), as to when communications involving representatives of a corporation are protected by the privilege. The Committee rejected limiting the privilege to members of the "control group" and added as subparagraph (a)(4) a definition for "representative of the client" that includes within the privilege disclosures not only of the client and the client's formal spokesperson, but also employees who are specifically authorized to communicate to the lawyer concerning a legal matter. The word "specifically" is intended to preclude a general authorization from the client for the client's employees to communicate under the cloak of the privilege, but is intended to allow the client, as related to a specific matter, to authorize the client's employees as "representatives" to disclose information to the lawyer as to that specific matter with confidence that the disclosures will remain within the lawyer-client privilege.

A "representative" of the lawyer need not be directly paid by the lawyer as long as the representative meets the requirement of being engaged to assist the lawyer in providing legal services. Thus, a person paid directly by the client but working under the control and direction of the lawyer for the purposes of providing legal services satisfies the requirements of subparagraph (a)(3). Similarly, a representative of the client who may be an independent contractor, such as an independent accountant, consultant or person providing other services, is a representative of the client for purposes of subparagraph (a)(5) if such person has been engaged to provide services reasonably related to the subject matter of the legal services or whose service is necessary to provide such service.

The client is entitled not only to refuse to disclose the confidential communication, but also to prevent disclosure by the lawyer or others who were involved in the conference or learned, without the knowledge of the client, the content of the confidential communication. Problems of waiver are dealt with by Rule 507.

Under subparagraph (b) communications among the various people involved in the legal matter, relating to the providing of legal services, are all privileged, except for communications between clients. Those are privileged only if they are part of a conference with others involved in legal services.

Subparagraph (c) allows the "successor, trustee, or similar representative of a corporation, association, or other organization, whether or not in existence" to claim the privilege. Where there is a dispute as to which of several persons has claims to the rights of a previously existing entity, the court will be required to determine from the facts which entity's claim is most consistent with the purposes of this rule.

The Committee considered and rejected an exception to the rule for communications in furtherance of a tort. Disallowing the privilege where the lawyer's services are sought in furtherance of a crime or fraud is consistent with the trend in other states. The Committee considered extending the exception to include "intentional torts," but concluded that because of the broad range of conduct that may be found to be an intentional tort, such an exception would create undesirable ambiguities and uncertainties as to when the privilege applies.

The Committee felt that exceptions to the privilege should be specifically enumerated, and further endorsed the concept that in the area of exceptions, the rule should simply state that no privilege existed, rather than expressing the exception in terms of a "waiver" of the privilege. The Committee wanted to avoid any possible clashes with the common law concepts of "waiver."

Rule 505. Government Informer.

(a) Definitions.

(1) "Government" means the government of the United States, of any state, or of any subdivision of any state.

(2) "Informer" means any person who has furnished information to a law enforcement officer relating to or assisting in an investigation of a possible violation of law.

(3) "Law enforcement officer" includes

(A) peace officers;

(B) prosecutors;

(C) members of a legislative committee or its staff conducting an investigation; and

(D) members of a regulatory agency or its staff conducting an investigation.

(b) Statement of the Privilege. The government has a privilege to refuse to disclose the identity of an informer.

(c) Who May Claim the Privilege. The privilege may be claimed by counsel for the government or in the absence of counsel by another appropriate representative. The privilege may be claimed regardless of whether the information was furnished to an officer of the government claiming the privilege.

(d) Exceptions: No privilege exists under paragraph (b) in the following circumstances:

(1) Voluntary Disclosure. If the identity of the informer or the informer's interest in the subject matter of the informer's communication has been disclosed to those who would have cause to resent the communication by a holder of the privilege or by the informer's own action.

(2) Informer as Witness. The informer appears as a witness for the government.

(e) Testimony on Merits.

(1) In General. If it appears from the evidence in the case or from another showing by a party that an informer may be able to give testimony necessary to a fair determination of the issue of guilt or innocence in a criminal case or of a material issue on the merits of a civil case, whether or not the government is a party, and the government invokes a privilege, the judge may give the government an opportunity to show in camera facts relevant to determining whether the informer can, in fact, supply the testimony. The judge may make such orders regarding the procedures to be followed as are consistent with the spirit and purpose of this rule.

(2) Effect of Invoking Privilege. If the judge finds there is reasonable probability that the informer can give the testimony, and the government elects not to disclose the informer's identity, the judge, on motion of the defendant in a criminal case, shall dismiss the charges to which the testimony would relate. The judge may dismiss the charges on the judge's own motion. In a civil case, the judge may make any order that justice requires.

(3) Record for Appeal. Evidence submitted to the judge may be sealed and preserved to be made available to the appellate court in the event of an appeal, and the contents shall not otherwise be revealed without consent of the government.

(4) Right to be Present. All counsel and parties shall be permitted to be present at every stage of the proceedings under this subparagraph, except a showing in camera at which no counsel or party shall be permitted to be present.

(f)   Legality of Obtained Evidence.

(1) Requirements for Disclosure. The judge may require the disclosure of the identity of an informer if

(A)   information from the informer is relied upon to establish the legality of the means by which evidence was obtained; and

(B)   the party attacking the legality of obtaining the evidence makes a substantial preliminary showing that the law enforcement officer intentionally, knowingly or with reckless disregard for truth falsely swore that the information was received from an informer reasonably believed to be reliable or credible and that probable cause does not exist absent the information furnished by the informer.

(2) Process of Disclosure. The judge shall, at the request of the government, direct that the disclosure be made in camera. All counsel and parties concerned with the issue of legality shall be permitted to be present at every stage of the proceeding under this subparagraph, except at a disclosure in camera, at which no counsel or parties shall be permitted to be present. If disclosure of the identity of the informer is made in camera, the record thereof shall be sealed and preserved to be made available to the appellate court in the event of an appeal, and the contents shall not otherwise be revealed without consent of the government.

2011 Advisory Committee Note. – The language of this rule has been amended as part of the restyling of the Evidence Rules to make them more easily understood and to make style and terminology consistent throughout the

rules. These changes are intended to be stylistic only. There is no intent to change any result in any ruling on evidence admissibility.

ADVISORY COMMITTEE NOTE

Rule 505 incorporates the concept reflected in Roviaro v. United States, 353 U.S. 53, 1 L. Ed. 2d 639, 77 S. Ct. 623 (1957), that the government has a "privilege to withhold from disclosure the identity of persons who furnish information of violations of law to officers charged with the enforcement of that law." The Utah Supreme Court adopted the Roviaroapproach in State v. Forshee, 611 P.2d 1222 (Utah 1980).

Subparagraph (b) makes it clear that it is the government which holds the privilege rather than the informer, the witness, or the law enforcement officer. This is so even though the earlier Rule 36, Utah Rules of Evidence, (1971) was couched in language that suggested that it was the witness' privilege.

Subparagraph (c) allows the privilege to be claimed by counsel for the government or, in the absence of counsel, allows the court to determine who is "another appropriate representative" of the government for the purposes of claiming the privilege. Subparagraph (d) makes it clear that the privilege is lost if (1) the informer appears as a witness for the government, (2) the informer discloses his or her identity to the party opposed to the privilege, or (3) the government discloses the informer's identity to the party opposed to the privilege.

Subparagraph (d)(1) sets forth the test to be applied by the court in determining whether to allow the privilege or to require the government to elect to disclose the identity of the informer or to dismiss, in a criminal case. The rule contemplates discretion in the court to hold in camera hearings to determine whether the test is met and to seal and preserve any information disclosed in such hearings, for appellate review.

Subparagraph (d)(2) provides procedure in conformity with Franks v. Delaware, 438 U.S. 154, 57 L. Ed. 2d 667, 98 S. Ct. 2674 (1978), to be followed in a motion to suppress or similar proceeding where a party opposed to the privilege wishes to learn the identity of a confidential informant in order to attack the probable cause upon which the search was based.

Rule 506. Physician and Mental Health Therapist-Patient.

(a)   Definitions.

    (1)   "Patient" means a person who consults or is examined or interviewed by a physician or mental health therapist.

    (2)   "Physician" means a person licensed, or reasonably believed by the patient to be licensed, to practice medicine in any state.

    (3)   "Mental health therapist" means a person who

        (A)   is or is reasonably believed by the patient to be licensed or certified in any state as a physician, psychologist, clinical or certified social worker, marriage and family therapist, advanced practice registered nurse designated as a registered psychiatric mental health nurse specialist, or professional counselor; and

        (B)   is engaged in the diagnosis or treatment of a mental or emotional condition, including alcohol or drug addiction.

(b)   Statement of the Privilege. A patient has a privilege, during the patient's life, to refuse to disclose and to prevent any other person from disclosing information that is communicated in confidence to a physician or mental health therapist for the purpose of diagnosing or treating the patient. The privilege applies to:

    (1)   diagnoses made, treatment provided, or advice given by a physician or mental health therapist;

    (2)   information obtained by examination of the patient; and

    (3)   information transmitted among a patient, a physician or mental health therapist, and other persons who are participating in the diagnosis or treatment under the direction of the physician or mental health therapist.

Such other persons include guardians or members of the patient's family who are present to further the interest of the patient because they are reasonably necessary for the transmission of the communications, or participation in the diagnosis and treatment under the direction of the physician or mental health therapist.

(c) **Who May Claim the Privilege.** The privilege may be claimed by the patient, or the guardian or conservator of the patient. The person who was the physician or mental health therapist at the time of the communication is presumed to have authority during the life of the patient to claim the privilege on behalf of the patient.

(d) **Exceptions.** No privilege exists under paragraph (b) in the following circumstances:

(1) **Condition as Element of Claim or Defense.** For communications relevant to an issue of the physical, mental, or emotional condition of the patient:

(A) in any proceeding in which that condition is an element of any claim or defense, or

(B) after the patient's death, in any proceedings in which any party relies upon the condition as an element of the claim or defense;

(2) **Hospitalization for Mental Illness.** For communications relevant to an issue in proceedings to hospitalize the patient for mental illness, if the mental health therapist in the course of diagnosis or treatment has determined that the patient is in need of hospitalization; and

(3) **Court Ordered Examination.** For communications made in the course of, and pertinent to the purpose of, a court-ordered examination of the physical, mental, or emotional condition of a patient, whether a party or witness, unless the court in ordering the examination specifies otherwise.

2011 Advisory Committee Note. – The language of this rule has been amended as part of the restyling of the Evidence Rules to make them more easily understood and to make style and terminology consistent throughout the rules. These changes are intended to be stylistic only. There is no intent to change any result in any ruling on evidence admissibility.

ADVISORY COMMITTEE NOTE

Rule 506 is modeled after Rule 503 of the Uniform Rules of Evidence, and is intended to supersede Utah Code Ann. §§ 78-24-8(4) and 58-25a-8. There is no corresponding federal rule. By virtue of Rule 501, marriage and family therapists are not covered by this Rule.

The differences between existing § 78-24-8 and Rule 506 are as follows:

(1) Rule 506 specifically applies to psychotherapists and licensed psychologists, it being the opinion of the Committee that full disclosure of information by a patient in those settings is as critical as and as much to be encouraged as in the "physician" patient setting. The Utah Supreme Court requested that Rule 506 further apply to licensed clinical social workers. To meet this request, the Committee included such individuals within the definition of psychotherapists. Under Utah Code Ann. § 58-35-2(5), the practice of clinical social work "means the application of an established body of knowledge and professional skills in the practice of psychotherapy. . . ." Section 58-35-6 provides that "[n]o person may engage in the practice of clinical social work unless that person: (1) is licensed under this chapter as a certified social worker," has the requisite experience, and has passed an examination. Section 58-35-8(4) refers to licenses and certificates for "clinical social worker[s]." As a result of including clinical social workers, Rule 506 is intended to supplant Utah Code Ann. § 58-35-10 in total for all social workers.

(2) Rule 506 applies to both civil and criminal cases, whereas § 78-24-8 applies only to civil cases. The Committee was of the opinion that the considerations supporting the privilege apply in both.

(3) In the Committee's original recommendation to the Utah Supreme Court, the proposed Rule 506 granted protection only to confidential communications, but did not extend the privilege to observations made, diagnosis or treatment by the physician/psychotherapist. The Committee was of the opinion that while the traditional protection of the privilege should extend to confidential communications, as is the case in other traditional privileges, the interests of society in discovering the truth during the trial process outweigh any countervailing interests in extending the protection to observations made, diagnosis or treatment. However, the Supreme Court requested that the scope of the privilege be broadened to include information obtained by the physician or psychotherapist in the course of

diagnosis or treatment, whether obtained verbally from the patient or through the physician's or psychotherapist's observation or examination of the patient. The Court further requested that the privilege extend to diagnosis, treatment, and advice. To meet these requests, the Committee relied in part on language from the California evidentiary privileges involving physicians and psychotherapists. See Cal. Evid. Code §§ 992 and 1012. These features of the rule appear in subparagraphs (a)(4) and (b). The Committee also relied on language from Uniform Rule of Evidence 503.

Upon the death of the patient, the privilege ceases to exist.

The privilege extends to communications to the physician or psychotherapist from other persons who are acting in the interest of the patient, such as family members or others who may be consulted for information needed to help the patient.

The privilege includes those who are participating in the diagnosis and treatment under the direction of the physician or psychotherapist. For example, a certified social worker practicing under the supervision of a clinical social worker would be included. See Utah Code Ann. § 58-35-6.

The patient is entitled not only to refuse to disclose the confidential communication, but also to prevent disclosure by the physician or psychotherapist or others who were properly involved or others who overheard, without the knowledge of the patient, the confidential communication. Problems of waiver are dealt with by Rule 507.

The Committee felt that exceptions to the privilege should be specifically enumerated, and further endorsed the concept that in the area of exceptions, the rule should simply state that no privilege existed, rather than expressing the exception in terms of a "waiver" of the privilege. The Committee wanted to avoid any possible clashes with the common law concepts of "waiver."

The Committee did not intend this rule to limit or conflict with the health care data statutes listed in the Committee Note to Rule 501.

Rule 506 is not intended to override the child abuse reporting requirements contained in Utah Code Ann. § 62A-4-501 et seq.

The 1994 amendment to Rule 506 was primarily in response to legislation enacted during the 1994 Legislative General Session that changed the licensure requirements for certain mental health professionals. The rule now covers communications with additional licensed professionals who are engaged in treatment and diagnosis of mental or emotional conditions, specifically certified social workers, marriage and family therapists, specially designated advanced practice registered nurses and professional counselors.

Some mental health therapists use the term "client" rather than "patient," but for simplicity this rule uses only "patient."

The committee also combined the definition of confidential communication and the general rule section, but no particular substantive change was intended by the reorganization.

Rule 507. First Responder Peer Support.

(a) **Definitions.**

(a)(1) "Peer Support communication" means information that is communicated in confidence to a peer support team member for the purpose of providing peer support services, including but not limited to oral statements, written statements, notes, records, or reports.

(a)(2) "Peer support team member" means a person who is:

(a)(2)(A) designated as a peer support team member for first responders under UCA §78B-5-901 and

(a)(2)(B) providing peer support services in accordance with written guidelines required by UCA § 78B-5-901.

(a)(3) "Peer support team member" does not mean a person who was a witness or a party to an incident that prompted the delivery of the peer support services.

(b) **Statement of the Privilege.** A person receiving peer support services from a peer support team member has a privilege during the person's life, to refuse to disclose and toprevent any other person from disclosing peer support communications.

(c) Who May Claim the Privilege. The privilege may be claimed by the person who received the peer support services, or the guardian or conservator of the person who received the peer support services. A person who was a peer support team member at the time of the communication is presumed to have authority during the life of the person who received the peer support services to claim the privilege on behalf of the person who received the peer support services.

(d) Exceptions. No privilege exists under paragraph (b) for:

(d)(1) communication to a peer support team member that is evidence of actual or suspected child neglect or abuse;

(d)(2) communication to a peer support team member that is evidence a person receiving peer support services is a clear and immediate danger to the person's self or others,

(d)(3) communication to a peer support team member that establishes reasonable cause for the peer support team member to believe the person receiving peer support services is mentally or emotionally unfit for duty; or

(d)(4) communication to the peer support team member that is evidence that the person who is receiving the peer support services has committed a crime, plans to commit acrime, or intends to conceal a crime.

Rule 508. Environmental Self-Evaluation Privilege.

(a) Definitions.

(1) "Administrative proceeding" means an adjudicatory proceeding conducted by the department or other government entity with authority to enforce any environmental law, including any notice of violation proceeding, any department proceeding listed in Utah Code § 19-1-305, or any proceeding conducted pursuant to Title 63G, Chapter 4, Utah Code, Utah Administrative Procedures Act.

(2) "Department" means the Department of Environmental Quality.

(3) "Environmental audit report" means any document, information, report, finding, communication, note drawing, graph, chart, photograph, survey, suggestion, or opinion, whether in preliminary, draft, or final form, prepared as the result of or in response to an environmental self-evaluation.

(4) "Environmental law" means any requirement contained in Title 19 Utah Code, or in rules made under Title 19, Utah Code, or in any rules, orders, permits, licenses, or closure plans issued or approved by the department, or in any other provision or ordinance addressing protection of the environment.

(5) "Environmental self-evaluation" means a self-initiated assessment, audit, or review, not otherwise expressly required by an environmental law, that is performed to determine whether a person is in compliance with environmental laws. A person may perform an environmental self-evaluation through the use of employees or the use of outside consultants.

(6) "In camera review" means a confidential review in which only the court has access to the privileged information.

(7) "Judicial proceeding" means a civil proceeding.

(b)   Statement of the Privilege.

(1) A person for whom an environmental self-evaluation is conducted or for whom an environmental audit report is prepared has a privilege to refuse to disclose, and prevent any other person from disclosing, an environmental audit report.

(2) The existence of an environmental audit report, but not its content, is subject to discovery but is not admissible in an administrative or judicial proceeding.

(3)   Use of an environmental audit report in a criminal proceeding does not waive or eliminate the privilege in an administrative or civil proceeding.

(c)   Who May Claim the Privilege. The privilege may be claimed by

(1)   the person for whom an environmental self-evaluation is conducted or for whom an environmental audit report is prepared; and

(2)   that person's guardian, conservator, personal representative, trustee, or successor in interest.

(d)   Exceptions to the Privilege. The privilege does not apply in the following circumstances:

(1)   Waiver.

(A)   If the person for whom the audit report was prepared expressly waives the privilege;

(B)   Regardless of who prepared the environmental audit report, only the person for whom the environmental audit report was prepared can waive the environmental self-evaluation privilege;

(C)   If that person is a corporation, company, or other business entity, the power to waive the privilege is limited to the officers and directors who have the requisite management authority to act for the entity.

(2)   Fraud. If the privilege is being asserted for a fraudulent purpose;

(3)   Avoidance. If the environmental audit report was prepared to avoid disclosure of information in a compliance investigation or proceeding that was already underway and known to the person asserting the privilege;

(4) Danger to Public Health or Environment. If the information contained in the environmental audit report must be disclosed to avoid a clear and impending danger to public health or the environment outside of the facility property;

(5) Failure to Address Noncompliance.

(A) If the environmental audit report conclusively shows that the person for whom the environmental audit report was prepared is not or was not in compliance with an environmental law and after the environmental audit report the person did not initiate appropriate efforts to achieve compliance with the environmental law within a reasonable amount of time.

(B) If an environmental audit report shows noncompliance with more than one environmental law, or if the noncompliance will require substantial resources to achieve compliance, and the person does not demonstrate that appropriate efforts to achieve compliance were or are being taken by instituting a comprehensive program that establishes a phased schedule of actions to be taken to bring the person into compliance within a reasonable amount of time;

(6) Required by Law. If the document or information is specifically required to be available or furnished to a regulatory agency by any environmental law or any other law or rule;

(7) Obtained by Department. If the information is obtained by the department through observation, sampling, or monitoring;

(8) Independent Source. If the information is obtained through any source independent of the voluntary environmental self-evaluation.

(e) In Camera Review.

(1) The person seeking disclosure of an environmental audit report shall request an in camera review of the audit report by a court of record.

(2) During in camera review, the party seeking disclosure of the environmental audit report may not have access to the environmental audit report.

(3) (A) If the court of record determines that part of an environmental audit report is not privileged, the court shall order the disclosure of the non-privileged portions of the environmental audit report.

(B) The privileged portions of the environmental audit report may not be disclosed.

(f)   Burden of Proof.

(1) The person asserting the environmental self-evaluation privilege has the burden of establishing a prima facie case of privilege.

(2) The person seeking disclosure of an environmental audit report has the burden of proving that the environmental audit report is not privileged.

(g)   Other Privileges Not Affected. Nothing in this rule:

(1) limits, waives, or abrogates the scope or nature of any other statutory or common law privilege; or

(2) limits, waives, or abrogates the department's authority to obtain or use documents or information that the department is required to have under federal law to obtain delegation of a federal program.

(h)   Scope of Rule. This rule applies to all administrative and judicial proceedings commenced on or after March 21, 1995.

2011 Advisory Committee Note. – The language of this rule has been amended as part of the restyling of the Evidence Rules to make them more easily understood and to make style and terminology consistent throughout the

rules. These changes are intended to be stylistic only. There is no intent to change any result in any ruling on evidence admissibility.

Rule 509. News Reporters.

(a)   Definitions.

(1) "News reporter" means a publisher, editor, reporter or other similar person gathering information for the primary purpose of disseminating news to the public and any newspaper, magazine, or other periodical publication, press association or wire service, radio station, television station, satellite broadcast, cable system or other organization with whom that person is connected.

(2) "Confidential source information" means the name or any other information likely to lead directly to the disclosure of the identity of a person who gives information to a news reporter with a reasonable expectation of confidentiality.

(3) "Confidential unpublished news information" means information, other than confidential source information, that is gathered by a news reporter on condition of confidentiality. This includes notes, outtakes, photographs, tapes or other data that are maintained by the news reporter or by the organization or entity on whose behalf the reporter was acting to the extent such records include information that was provided on condition of confidentiality.

(4) "Other unpublished news information" means information, other than confidential unpublished news information, that is gathered by a news reporter. This includes notes, outtakes, photographs, tapes or other data that are maintained by the news reporter or by the organization or entity on whose behalf the reporter was acting.

(b)   Statement of the Privilege for Confidential Source Information. A news reporter or confidential source has a privilege to refuse to disclose — and to prevent any other person from disclosing — confidential source information, unless the person seeking the information demonstrates by clear and convincing evidence that disclosure is necessary to prevent substantial injury or death.

(c)   Statement of the Privilege for Confidential Unpublished News Information. A news reporter has a privilege to refuse to disclose confidential unpublished news information, unless the person seeking the information demonstrates a need for that information that substantially outweighs the interest of a continued free flow of information to news reporters.

(d)   Statement of the Privilege for Other Unpublished News Information. A news reporter has a privilege to refuse to disclose other unpublished news information if the person claiming the privilege demonstrates that the interest of a continued free flow of information to news reporters outweighs the need for disclosure.

(e)   Who May Claim. The privileges may be claimed, as applicable, by the news reporter, the organization or entity on whose behalf the news reporter was acting, the confidential source, the news reporter's or confidential source's guardian or conservator or the personal representative of a deceased news reporter or confidential source.

(f)   In Camera Review. If the court makes an initial determination that information which is claimed to be privileged under this rule should be disclosed, the court shall conduct an in camera review of that information before making a final determination requiring disclosure.

2011 Advisory Committee Note. – The language of this rule has been amended as part of the restyling of the Evidence Rules to make them more easily understood and to make style and terminology consistent throughout the rules. These changes are intended to be stylistic only. There is no intent to change any result in any ruling on evidence admissibility.

ADVISORY COMMITTEE NOTE

Protection of news gathering and dissemination has roots in the First Amendment of the United States Constitution. See Branzburg v. Hayes, 408 U.S. 665 (1972); Redding v. Jacobsen, 639 P.2d 503 (Utah 1981). Since Branzburg, there has been an increasing but somewhat inconsistent development of the law concerning this privilege. Indeed, the extent of a federally-recognized privilege remains unclear. Many states have addressed the subject with legislation such that there is substantial variation in how the privilege may operate in different jurisdictions. The committee proposed this rule to address any uncertainty that may exist under Utah law and to provide for uniformity in the recognition of the privilege by Utah courts.

Although recognition of a reporter's privilege, as with all privileges, may limit the disclosure of specific facts in developing an evidentiary record in a particular case, the law has long recognized that some societal needs and values outweigh disclosure. To this end, the reporter's privilege has been recognized as important in assuring a continued free flow of information to those who gather and publish the news. See Silkwood v. KerrMcGee Corp., 563 F. 2d 433 (10th Cir. 1977); Bottomly v. Leucadia National Corp., 24 Media L. Rep. 2118, 1996 U.S. Dist LEXIS 14760 (D. Utah, July 2, 1996) (Boyce, J.); Edward L. Carter, Reporter's Privilege in Utah, 18 BYU Journal of Public Law 163 (2003).

This rule is intended to clarify the legal standard to be applied in determining whether a news reporter may be compelled to disclose information gathered in the course of reporting the news. The rule requires the court to consider the interests of the person seeking disclosure and the interests of the free flow of information to news reporters. In Silkwood, the court recognized that, in balancing the interests, the court should consider as factors (1) whether the party seeking the information has attempted independently to obtain the information, (2) whether the information being sought goes to the heart of the matter, (3) whether the information is of certain relevance, and (4) the type of controversy. These are factors that should be considered by the court in weighing whether the need for the information outweighs the interest of a continued free flow of information to news reporters. As the law in this area continues to develop, the court should consider other factors found to influence the open and free flow of information that is vital to our culture and form of government. The rule incorporates a relatively broad and flexible definition of news reporter to accommodate the ever-changing methods of expression and publication. While there are not many "lone pamphleteers" still functioning, they may have modern-day counterparts on the internet.

Because of the requirement that the court weigh the relevant criteria in deciding whether to require disclosure, the rule provides flexibility to address the different circumstances, many unpredictable, that may arise. The rule provides the greatest protection to the name of a confidential source or other information that would lead directly to the disclosure of the source's identity. See Subparagraph (b). The term "substantial injury" as used in Subparagraph (b) is not limited to bodily injury. For information obtained on condition of confidentiality, the rule requires the person seeking the information to demonstrate that under the balancing test set forth in Silkwood, and other relevant criteria the court may consider, the need for the information "substantially" outweighs the interests of society in protecting the information from disclosure. See Subparagraph (c). For other unpublished news information, however, the person claiming the privilege must demonstrate that the need to encourage the free flow of information outweighs the need for disclosure. See Subparagraph (d).

Although the rule does not contain exceptions to the privilege, recognizing that in most cases those issues will be resolved by applying the balancing test, the rule is not intended to limit or protect from disclosure those classes of information that by statute or other established law must be disclosed. See, e.g., Utah Code Annotated § 62A-4a-401 et seq. regarding child abuse reporting requirements, and §76-5-111.1 regarding vulnerable adult abuse reporting requirements.

Finally, subparagraph (f) adds additional protection to assure that a claimed need for information to be disclosed is not abused. Once the court determines that the party seeking disclosure has met the requirements under the balancing test, the court is then required to review the information in camera to confirm that the represented need for the information in fact balances in favor of disclosure. If upon review of the information the court is satisfied that the balance favors disclosure, the court may make a final determination ordering the information be disclosed. This additional protection is not intended to infringe on the court's general discretionary authority to review evidence in camera whenever it is deemed necessary.

Rule 510. Miscellaneous Matters.

(a) **Waiver of Privilege.** A person who holds a privilege under these rules waives the privilege if the person or a previous holder of the privilege:

> **(1)** voluntarily discloses or consents to the disclosure of any significant part of the matter or communication, or

(2) fails to take reasonable precautions against inadvertent disclosure.

This privilege is not waived if the disclosure is itself a privileged communication.

(b) **Inadmissibility of Disclosed Information.** Evidence of a statement or other disclosure of privileged matter is not admissible against the holder of the privilege if disclosure was compelled erroneously or made without opportunity to claim the privilege.

(c) **Comment or Inference Not Permitted.** The claim of privilege, whether in the present proceeding or upon a prior occasion, is not a proper subject of comment by judge or counsel. No inference may be drawn from any claim of privilege.

(d) **Claiming Privilege Without the Jury's Knowledge.** To the extent practicable, jury cases shall be conducted to allow claims of privilege to be made without the jury's knowledge.

(e) **Jury Instruction.** Upon request, any party against whom the jury might draw an adverse inference from the claim of privilege is entitled to a jury instruction that no inference may be drawn from that claim of privilege.

(f) **Privilege Against Self-Incrimination in Civil Cases.** In a civil case, the provisions of paragraph (c)-(e) do not apply when the privilege against self-incrimination has been invoked.

2011 Advisory Committee Note. – The language of this rule has been amended as part of the restyling of the Evidence Rules to make them more easily understood and to make style and terminology consistent throughout the rules. These changes are intended to be stylistic only. There is no intent to change any result in any ruling on evidence admissibility.

ADVISORY COMMITTEE NOTE

The subject matter of Rule 510 was previously included in Utah Rules of Evidence 37, 38, 39 and 40. The language recommended by the Committee, however, is largely that of proposed Federal Rules 511, 512 and 513, rules not included among those adopted by Congress.

Proposed Federal Rule 511 became Rule 510(a), replacing Rule 37. Proposed Federal Rule 512 became Rule 510(b), replacing Rule 38. Proposed Federal Rule 513 became Rule 510(c), replacing Rule 39. No replacement was adopted for Rule 40 since the Committee determined that the subject matter of that rule need not be covered by a rule of evidence.

Subparagraph (a). Since the purpose of evidentiary privileges is the protection of some societal interest or confidential relationship, the privilege should end when the purpose is no longer served because the holder of the privilege has allowed disclosure or made disclosure. For the same reason, although Rule 37 required a knowing waiver of the privilege, Rule 510(a) as drafted does not require such knowledge. A stranger to the communication may testify to an otherwise privileged communication, if the participants have failed to take reasonable precautions to preserve privacy.

Subparagraph (b). Once disclosure of privileged matter has occurred, although confidentiality cannot be restored, the purpose of the privilege may still be served in some instances by preventing use of the evidence against the holder of the privilege. For that reason, privileged matter may still be excluded when the disclosure was not voluntary or was made without an opportunity to claim the privilege.

Subparagraph (c).

(1) Allowing inferences to be drawn from the invocation of a privilege might undermine the interest or relationship the privilege was designed to protect.

(2) For the same reason, the invocation of a privilege should not be revealed to the jury. Doing so might also result in unwarranted emphasis on the exclusion of the privileged matter.

(3) Whether to seek an instruction is left to the judgment of counsel for the party against whom the inference might be drawn. If requested, such an instruction is a matter of right.

(4) The provisions of subparagraph (c)(4) are not intended to alter the common law rules as to inferences that may be drawn or as to when a party may comment or be entitled to a jury instruction when the privilege has been invoked.

Rule 511. Insurance Regulators.

(a) Definitions.

(1) "Commissioner" has the same meaning as set forth in Utah Code §31A-1- 301.

(2) "Department" has the same meaning as set forth in Utah Code §31A-1- 301.

(3) "NAIC" means the National Association of Insurance Commissioners.

(4) "Confidential Information" means information, documents, and copies of these that are obtained by or disclosed to the Commissioner or any other person in the course of an examination or investigation made under Utah Code §31A-16-107.5, §31A-16a-107 and all information reported under Utah Code §§31A-16-105 and 31A-16a-105.

(b) Statement of the privilege for Confidential Information.

(1) The Commissioner and the Department have a privilege to refuse to disclose in a private civil action Confidential Information that is within the possession or control of the Commissioner and the Department, unless the Commissioner has determined that the Confidential Information may be released pursuant to Utah Code §§31A-16-109 and 31A-16a-108.

(2) The NAIC has a privilege to refuse to disclose in a private civil action Confidential Information that is within the possession or control of the NAIC.

(c) Who may claim. The privilege may be claimed solely by the Commissioner, representatives of the Department, or representatives of the NAIC.

(d) Circumstances not constituting waiver. No waiver of any applicable privilege shall occur as a result of disclosure of documents, materials, or information to the Commissioner under Utah Code §§31A-16-109 and 31A-16a-108 or as a result of sharing documents, materials, or information under Utah Code §§31A-16-109(3) and 31A-16a-108(3).

Effective December 1, 2017

2017 Committee Note. The 2017 amendments reflect 2017 legislative changes to the underlying statute. Minor style and other non-substantive edits were also made.

Article VI Witnesses

Rule 601. General Rules of Competency

(a)   Every person is competent to be a witness unless these rules provide otherwise.

(b)   In an action for the declarant's wrongful death, a statement of the declarant is admissible against the plaintiff notwithstanding the hearsay rule.

(c)   In an action against the declarant's estate, the declarant's statement is admissible notwithstanding the hearsay rule if it was made at a time when the matter had been recently perceived by the declarant and while the declarant's recollection was clear unless it was made under circumstances indicating its lack of trustworthiness.

2011 Advisory Committee Note. – The language of this rule has been amended as part of the restyling of the Evidence Rules to make them more easily understood and to make style and terminology consistent throughout the rules. These changes are intended to be stylistic only. There is no intent to change any result in any ruling on evidence admissibility.

ADVISORY COMMITTEE NOTE

Subdivision (a) of the rule generally embodies, in simpler terms, the substance of Rules 7 and 17, Utah Rules of Evidence (1971). The effect will be to displace the decisions of the Utah Supreme Court applying Mansfield's Rule to a contest as to the legitimacy of children. Cf. Lopes v. Lopes, 30 Utah 2d 393, 518 P.2d 687 (1974); Miller v. Marticorena, 531 P.2d 487 (1975).

Rule 601 departs from the federal rule by adding two paragraphs to treat the problem of litigation involving deceased persons. The rule supersedes the Utah "Dead Man" statute, Utah Code Annotated, § 78-24-2 (1953), which is no longer operable. However, subparagraph (b) allows a decedent's hearsay statements to be received as an admission against the plaintiff in a wrongful death action. Subparagraph (c) authorizes the admission of a relevant hearsay statement of a deceased when offered in a suit against the estate of the deceased declarant. These two paragraphs have been taken from Sections 1227 and 1261 of the California Evidence Code. They have been placed in Rule 601 because they compensate for the "Dead Man" statute which related to competency and because to place the provisions in the hearsay section of the rules would disturb the correlation between the Utah rules format and the Federal rules. These two subparagraphs should also be read in connection with the other hearsay exceptions in Article VIII, in that statements not within Rule 601 may otherwise be admissible under other hearsay exceptions.

Rule 602. Need for Personal Knowledge

A witness may testify to a matter only if evidence is introduced sufficient to support a finding that the witness has personal knowledge of the matter. Evidence to prove personal knowledge may consist of the witness's own testimony. This rule does not apply to a witness's expert testimony under Rule 703.

2011 Advisory Committee Note. – The language of this rule has been amended as part of the restyling of the Evidence Rules to make them more easily understood and to make style and terminology consistent throughout the rules. These changes are intended to be stylistic only. There is no intent to change any result in any ruling on evidence admissibility. This rule is the federal rule, verbatim.

ADVISORY COMMITTEE NOTE

This rule is the federal rule, verbatim, and embodies the substance of Rule 10, Utah Rules of Evidence (1971).

Rule 603. Oath or Affirmation to Testify Truthfully

Before testifying, a witness must give an oath or affirmation to testify truthfully. It must be in a form designed to impress that duty on the witness's conscience.

2011 Advisory Committee Note. – The language of this rule has been amended as part of the restyling of the Evidence Rules to make them more easily understood and to make style and terminology consistent throughout the rules. These changes are intended to be stylistic only. There is no intent to change any result in any ruling on evidence admissibility. This rule is the federal rule, verbatim.

ADVISORY COMMITTEE NOTE

This rule is the federal rule, verbatim. The oath or affirmation need not be in any special form but only such as to awaken the conscience of the witness and impress the witness with the duty to testify truthfully. The rule is a modified version of Rule 18, Utah Rules of Evidence (1971).

Rule 604. Interpreter

An interpreter must be qualified and must give an oath or affirmation to make a true translation.

Advisory Committee Note. – The language of this rule has been amended as part of the restyling of the Evidence Rules to make them more easily understood and to make style and terminology consistent throughout the rules. These changes are intended to be stylistic only. There is no intent to change any result in any ruling on evidence admissibility. This rule is the federal rule, verbatim.

ADVISORY COMMITTEE NOTE

This rule is the federal rule, verbatim, and embodies the substance of Rule 17, Utah Rules of Evidence (1971).

Rule 605. Judge's Competency as a Witness

The presiding judge may not testify as a witness at the trial. A party need not object to preserve the issue.

2011 Advisory Committee Note. – The language of this rule has been amended as part of the restyling of the Evidence Rules to make them more easily understood and to make style and terminology consistent throughout the rules. These changes are intended to be stylistic only. There is no intent to change any result in any ruling on evidence admissibility. This rule is the federal rule, verbatim.

ADVISORY COMMITTEE NOTE

This rule is the federal rule, verbatim, and is comparable to Rule 42, Utah Rules of Evidence (1971) except that under Rule 42, it is incumbent upon a party to object to the judge testifying. Compare Utah Code Annotated, § 78-24-3 (1953).

Rule 606. Juror's Competency as a Witness

(a)   **At the Trial**. A juror may not testify as a witness before the other jurors at the trial. If a juror is called to testify, the court must give a party an opportunity to object outside the jury's presence.

(b)   **During an Inquiry into the Validity of a Verdict or Indictment.**

(1)   **Prohibited Testimony or Other Evidence.** During an inquiry into the validity of a verdict or indictment, a juror may not testify about any statement made or incident that occurred during the jury's deliberations; the effect of anything on that juror's or another juror's vote; or any juror's mental processes concerning the verdict or indictment. The court may not receive a juror's affidavit or evidence of a juror's statement on these matters.

(2) Exceptions. A juror may testify about whether:

   (A) extraneous prejudicial information was improperly brought to the jury's attention; or

   (B) an outside influence was improperly brought to bear on any juror.

2011 Advisory Committee Note. – The language of this rule has been amended as part of the restyling of the Evidence Rules to make them more easily understood and to make style and terminology consistent throughout the rules. These changes are intended to be stylistic only. There is no intent to change any result in any ruling on evidence admissibility.

ADVISORY COMMITTEE NOTE

This rule is the federal rule, verbatim, and comports with Rules 41 and 44, Utah Rules of Evidence (1971), and Utah case law, State v. Gee, 28 Utah 2d 96, 498 P.2d 662 (1972).

Rule 607. Who May Impeach a Witness

Any party, including the party that called the witness, may attack the witness's credibility.

Advisory Committee Note. – The language of this rule has been amended as part of the restyling of the Evidence Rules to make them more easily understood and to make style and terminology consistent throughout the rules. These changes are intended to be stylistic only. There is no intent to change any result in any ruling on evidence admissibility. This rule is the federal rule, verbatim.

ADVISORY COMMITTEE NOTE

This rule is the federal rule, verbatim, and is similar to Rule 20, Utah Rules of Evidence (1971)

Rule 608. A Witness's Character for Truthfulness or Untruthfulness

(a)   Reputation or Opinion Evidence. A witness's credibility may be attacked or supported by testimony about the witness's reputation for having a character for truthfulness or untruthfulness, or by testimony in the form of an opinion about that character. But evidence of truthful character is admissible only after the witness's character for truthfulness has been attacked.

(b)   Specific Instances of Conduct. Except for a criminal conviction under Rule 609, extrinsic evidence is not admissible to prove specific instances of a witness's conduct in order to attack or support the witness's character for truthfulness. But the court may, on cross-examination, allow them to be inquired into if they are probative of the character for truthfulness or untruthfulness of:

    (1)   the witness; or

    (2)   another witness whose character the witness being cross-examined has testified about.

By testifying on another matter, a witness does not waive any privilege against self-incrimination for testimony that relates only to the witness's character for truthfulness.

(c)   Evidence of Bias. Bias, prejudice or any motive to misrepresent may be shown to impeach the witness either by examination of the witness or by other evidence.

2011 Advisory Committee Note. – The language of this rule has been amended as part of the restyling of the Evidence Rules to make them more easily understood and to make style and terminology consistent throughout the rules. These changes are intended to be stylistic only. There is no intent to change any result in any ruling on evidence admissibility.

ADVISORY COMMITTEE NOTE

This amendment is in order to be consistent with changes made to the Federal Rule.

Subdivisions (a) and (b) are the federal rule, verbatim, and are comparable to Rules 22 and 6, Utah Rules of Evidence (1971), except to the extent that Subdivision (a) limits such evidence to credibility for truthfulness or untruthfulness. Rule 22(c), Utah Rules of Evidence (1971) allowed a broader attack on the character of a witness as to truth, honesty and integrity.

This rule should be read in conjunction with Rule 405. Subdivision (b) allows, in the discretion of the court on cross-examination, inquiry into specific instances of the witness's conduct relative to his character for truthfulness or untruthfulness or specific instances of conduct of a person as to whom the witness has provided character testimony. See, State v. Adams, 26 Utah 2d 377, 489 P.2d 1191 (1971). Attack upon a witness's credibility by specific instances of character other than conviction of a crime is inadmissible under current Utah law. Cf. Bullock v. Ungricht, 538 P.2d 190 (Utah 1975); Rule 47, Utah Rules of Evidence (1971). Allowing cross-examination of a witness as to specific instances affecting character for truthfulness is new to Utah practice and in accord with the decision in Michelson v. United States, 335 U.S. 469 (1948). The cross-examination of a character witness as to specific instances of conduct which the character witness may have heard about concerning the person whose character is placed in evidence has been sanctioned by a prior decision, State v. Watts, 639 P.2d 158 (Utah 1981).

The rule is subject to a witness invoking the statutory privilege against degradation contained in Utah Code Annotated, Section 78-24-9 (1953). See, In re Peterson, 15 Utah 2d 27, 386 P.2d 726 (1963). The privilege, however, may be subject to limitation to accommodate an accused's right of confrontation. Cf. Davis v. Alaska, 415 U.S. 308 (1974).

Subdivision (c) is Rule 608(c), Military Rules of Evidence, verbatim.

Rule 609. Impeachment by Evidence of a Criminal Conviction

(a) **In General.** The following rules apply to attacking a witness's character for truthfulness by evidence of a criminal conviction:

(1) for a crime that, in the convicting jurisdiction, was punishable by death or by imprisonment for more than one year, the evidence:

    (A) must be admitted, subject to Rule 403, in a civil case or in a criminal case in which the witness is not a defendant; and

    (B) must be admitted in a criminal case in which the witness is a defendant, if the probative value of the evidence outweighs its prejudicial effect to that defendant; and

(2) for any crime regardless of the punishment, the evidence must be admitted if the court can readily determine that establishing the elements of the crime required proving — or the witness's admitting — a dishonest act or false statement.

(b) Limit on Using the Evidence After 10 Years. This subdivision (b) applies if more than 10 years have passed since the witness's conviction or release from confinement for it, whichever is later. Evidence of the conviction is admissible only if:

its probative value, supported by specific facts and circumstances, substantially outweighs its prejudicial effect; and

the proponent gives an adverse party reasonable written notice of the intent to use it so that the party has a fair opportunity to contest its use.

(c) Effect of a Pardon, Annulment, or Certificate of Rehabilitation. Evidence of a conviction is not admissible if:

(1) the conviction has been the subject of a pardon, annulment, certificate of rehabilitation, or other equivalent procedure based on a finding that the person has been rehabilitated, and the person has not been convicted of a later crime punishable by death or by imprisonment for more than one year; or

(2) the conviction has been the subject of a pardon, annulment, or other equivalent procedure based on a finding of innocence.

(d) **Juvenile Adjudications**. Evidence of a juvenile adjudication is admissible under this rule only if:

(1) it is offered in a criminal case;

(2) the adjudication was of a witness other than the defendant;

(3) an adult's conviction for that offense would be admissible to attack the adult's credibility; and

(4) admitting the evidence is necessary to fairly determine guilt or innocence.

(e) **Pendency of an Appeal**. A conviction that satisfies this rule is admissible even if an appeal is pending. Evidence of the pendency is also admissible.

2011 Advisory Committee Note. – The language of this rule has been amended as part of the restyling of the Evidence Rules to make them more easily understood and to make style and terminology consistent throughout the rules. These changes are intended to be stylistic only. There is no intent to change any result in any ruling on evidence admissibility. This rule is the federal rule, verbatim.

ADVISORY COMMITTEE NOTE

This rule is the federal rule, verbatim, and changes Utah law by granting the court discretion in convictions not involving dishonesty or false statement to refuse to admit the evidence if it would be prejudicial to the defendant. Current Utah law mandates the admission of such evidence. State v. Bennett, 30 Utah 2d 343, 517 P.2d 1029 (1973); State v. Van Dam, 554 P.2d 1324 (Utah 1976); State v. McCumber, 622 P.2d 353 (Utah 1980).

There is presently no provision in Utah law similar to Subsection (d).

The pendency of an appeal does not render a conviction inadmissible. This is in accord with Utah case law. State v. Crawford, 60 Utah 6, 206 P. 717 (1922).

This rule is identical to Rule 609 of the Federal Rules of Evidence. The 1990 amendments to the federal rule made two changes in the rule. The comment to the federal rule accurately reflects the Committee's view of the purpose of the amendments.

Rule 610. Religious Beliefs or Opinions

Evidence of a witness's religious beliefs or opinions is not admissible to attack or support the witness's credibility.

2011 Advisory Committee Note. – The language of this rule has been amended as part of the restyling of the Evidence Rules to make them more easily understood and to make style and terminology consistent throughout the rules. These changes are intended to be stylistic only. There is no intent to change any result in any ruling on evidence admissibility. This rule is the federal rule, verbatim.

ADVISORY COMMITTEE NOTE

This rule is the federal rule, verbatim, and is in accord with Rule 20, Utah Rules of Evidence (1971).

Rule 611. Mode and Order of Examining Witnesses and Presenting Evidence

(a)   Control by the Court; Purposes. The court should exercise reasonable control over the mode and order of examining witnesses and presenting evidence so as to:

(1)   make those procedures effective for determining the truth;

(2) avoid wasting time; and

(3) protect witnesses from harassment or undue embarrassment.

(b) **Scope of Cross-Examination**. Cross-examination should not go beyond the subject matter of the direct examination and matters affecting the witness's credibility. The court may allow inquiry into additional matters as if on direct examination.

(c) **Leading Questions.** Leading questions should not be used on direct examination except as necessary to develop the witness's testimony. Ordinarily, the court should allow leading questions:

(1) on cross-examination; and

(2) when a party calls a hostile witness, an adverse party, or a witness identified with an adverse party.

2011 Advisory Committee Note. – The language of this rule has been amended as part of the restyling of the Evidence Rules to make them more easily understood and to make style and terminology consistent throughout the rules. These changes are intended to be stylistic only. There is no intent to change any result in any ruling on evidence admissibility. This rule is the federal rule, verbatim.

ADVISORY COMMITTEE NOTE

This rule is the federal rule, verbatim, and restates the inherent power of the court to control the judicial process. Cf. Vanderpool v. Hargis, 23 Utah 2d 210, 461 P.2d 56 (1969). There was no comparable provision to Subsection (b) in Utah Rules of Evidence (1971), but it is comparable to current Utah case law and practice. Degnan, Non-Rules Evidence Law: Cross-Examination, 6 Utah L. Rev. 323 (1959). Subsection (c) is comparable to current Utah practice. Cf. Rule 43(b), Utah Rules of Civil Procedure.

Rule 612. Writing Used to Refresh a Witness's Memory

(a) **Scope.** This rule gives an adverse party certain options when a witness uses a writing to refresh memory:

(1) while testifying; or

(2) before testifying, if the court decides that justice requires the party to have those options.

(b) **Adverse Party's Options; Deleting Unrelated Matter.** An adverse party is entitled to have the writing produced at the hearing, to inspect it, to cross-examine the witness about it, and to introduce in evidence any portion that relates to the witness's testimony. If the producing party claims that the writing includes unrelated matter, the court must examine the writing in camera, delete any unrelated portion, and order that the rest be delivered to the adverse party. Any portion deleted over objection must be preserved for the record.

(c) **Failure to Produce or Deliver the Writing.** If a writing is not produced or is not delivered as ordered, the court may issue any appropriate order. But if the prosecution does not comply in a criminal case, the court must strike the witness's testimony or — if justice so requires — declare a mistrial.

Advisory Committee Note. – The language of this rule has been amended as part of the restyling of the Evidence Rules to make them more easily understood and to make style and terminology consistent throughout the rules. These changes are intended to be stylistic only. There is no intent to change any result in any ruling on evidence admissibility.

ADVISORY COMMITTEE NOTE

This rule generally comports with current Utah practice.

Rule 613. Witness's Prior Statement

(a)   Showing or Disclosing the Statement During Examination. When examining a witness about the witness's prior statement, a party need not show it or disclose its contents to the witness. But the party must, on request, show it or disclose its contents to an adverse party's attorney.

(b)   Extrinsic Evidence of a Prior Inconsistent Statement. Extrinsic evidence of a witness's prior inconsistent statement is admissible only if the witness is given an opportunity to explain or deny the statement and an adverse party is given an opportunity to examine the witness about it, or if justice so requires. This subdivision (b) does not apply to an opposing party's statement under Rule 801(d)(2).

2011 Advisory Committee Note. – The language of this rule has been amended as part of the restyling of the Evidence Rules to make them more easily understood and to make style and terminology consistent throughout the rules. These changes are intended to be stylistic only. There is no intent to change any result in any ruling on evidence admissibility. This rule is the federal rule, verbatim.

ADVISORY COMMITTEE NOTE

This rule is the federal rule, verbatim. Subsection (a) abandons the position in Queens Case, 129 English Reports 976 (1820), requiring that the cross-examiner, prior to examining a witness about his written statement, must first show the statement to the witness and is comparable to the substance of Rule 22(a), Utah Rules of Evidence (1971). The substance of Subsection (b) was formerly in Rule 22(b), Utah Rules of Evidence (1971).

Rule 614. Court's Calling or Examining a Witness

(a)   Calling. The court may call a witness on its own or at a party's request. Each party is entitled to cross-examine the witness.

(b)   Examining. The court may examine a witness regardless of who calls the witness.

(c) **Objections.** A party may object to the court's calling or examining a witness either at that time or at the next opportunity when the jury is not present.

2011 Advisory Committee Note. – The language of this rule has been amended as part of the restyling of the Evidence Rules to make them more easily understood and to make style and terminology consistent throughout the rules. These changes are intended to be stylistic only. There is no intent to change any result in any ruling on evidence admissibility. This rule is the federal rule, verbatim.

ADVISORY COMMITTEE NOTE

This rule is the federal rule, verbatim. Rule 614 is generally in accord with current Utah law and practice.

Rule 615. Excluding Witnesses

At a party's request, the court must order witnesses excluded so that they cannot hear other witnesses' testimony. Or the court may do so on its own. But this rule does not authorize excluding:

(a) a party who is a natural person;

(b) an officer or employee of a party that is not a natural person, after being designated as the party's representative by its attorney;

(c) a person whose presence a party shows to be essential to presenting the party's claim or defense;

(d) a victim in a criminal or juvenile delinquency proceeding where the prosecutor agrees with the victim's presence;

(e)   a victim counselor while the victim is present unless the defendant establishes that the counselor is a material witness in that criminal or juvenile delinquency proceeding; or

(f)   a person authorized by statute to be present.

2011 Advisory Committee Note. – The language of this rule has been amended as part of the restyling of the Evidence Rules to make them more easily understood and to make style and terminology consistent throughout the rules. These changes are intended to be stylistic only. There is no intent to change any result in any ruling on evidence admissibility.

Rule 616. Statements Made During Custodial Interrogations.

(a)   Definitions.

(1) "Custodial interrogation" means questioning or other conduct by a law enforcement officer that is reasonably likely to elicit an incriminating response from a person and occurs when reasonable persons in the same circumstances would consider themselves in custody.

(2) "Electronic recording" means an audio recording or an audio-video recording that accurately records a custodial interrogation.

(3) "Law enforcement agency" means a governmental entity or person authorized by a governmental entity or by state law to enforce criminal laws or investigate suspected criminal activity. The term includes a nongovernmental entity that has been delegated the authority to enforce criminal laws or investigate suspected criminal activity.

(4) "Law enforcement officer" means a person described in Utah Code § 53-13-103(1).

(5) "Place of detention" means a facility or area owned or operated by a law enforcement agency where persons are detained in connection with criminal investigations or questioned about alleged criminal conduct. The term includes a law enforcement agency station, jail, holding cell, correctional or detention facility, police vehicle or any other stationary or mobile building owned or operated by a law enforcement agency.

(6) "Statement" means the same as in Rule 801(a).

(b)   Admissibility. Except as otherwise provided in Subsection (c) of this rule, evidence of a statement made by the defendant during a custodial interrogation in a place of detention shall not be admitted against the defendant in a felony criminal prosecution unless an electronic recording of the statement was made and is available at trial. This requirement is in addition to, and does not diminish, any other requirement regarding the admissibility of a person's statements.

(c)   Exceptions. Notwithstanding subsection (b), the court may admit a statement made under any of the following circumstances if the statement is otherwise admissible under the law:

(1) The statement was made prior to January 1, 2016;

(2) The statement was made during a custodial interrogation that occurred outside Utah and was conducted by officers of a jurisdiction outside Utah;

(3) The statement is offered for impeachment purposes only;

(4) The statement was a spontaneous statement made outside the course of a custodial interrogation or made during routine processing or booking of the person;

(5) Before or during a custodial interrogation, the person agreed to respond to questions only if his or her statements were not electronically recorded, provided that such agreement is electronically recorded or documented in writing;

(6) The law enforcement officers conducting the custodial interrogation in good faith failed to make an electronic recording because the officers inadvertently failed to operate the recording equipment properly, or without the knowledge of any of the officers the recording equipment malfunctioned or stopped operating;

(7) The law enforcement officers conducting or observing the custodial interrogation reasonably believed that the crime for which the person was being investigated was not a felony under Utah law;

(8) Substantial exigent circumstances existed that prevented or rendered unfeasible the making of an electronic recording of the custodial interrogation, or prevented its preservation and availability at trial; or

(9) The court finds:

    (A) The statement has substantial guarantees of trustworthiness and reliability equivalent to those of an electronic recording; and

    (B) Admitting the statement best serves the purposes of these rules and the interests of justice.

(d) Procedure to determine admissibility.

(1) **Notice**. If the prosecution intends to offer an unrecorded statement under an exception described in Subsection (c)(4) through (9) of this Rule, the prosecution must serve the defendant with written notice of an intent to rely on such an exception not later than 30 days before trial.

(2) **Instruction**. If the court admits into evidence a statement made during a custodial interrogation that was not electronically recorded under an exception described in Subsection (c)(4) through (9) of this Rule, the court, upon request of the defendant, may give cautionary instructions to the jury concerning the unrecorded statement.

2015 Advisory Committee Note – In 2008, the Utah Attorney General's Office, in cooperation with statewide law enforcement agencies, drafted a Best Practices Statement for Law Enforcement that recommended electronic recording of custodial interrogations. Since then, most agencies have adopted the Statement or their own policies to record custodial interviews. This rule is promulgated to bring statewide uniformity to the admissibility of statements made during custodial interrogations. See *State v. Perea*, 2013 UT 68, ¶ 130, 322 P.3d 624.

Several states have adopted requirements for recording custodial interviews, and the National Conference of Commissioners on Uniform State Law has approved and recommended for enactment a Uniform Electronic Recordation of Custodial Interrogations Act.

The benefits of recording custodial interrogations include "avoiding unwarranted claims of coercion"; preventing the use of "actual coercive tactics by police"; and demonstrating "the voluntariness of the confession, the context in which a particular statement was made, and . . . the actual content of the statement." *State v. James*, 858 P.2d 1012, 1018 (Utah Ct. App. 1993) (internal quotation marks omitted). Recordings assist the fact-finder and protect police officers and agencies from false claims of coercion and misconduct. *Perea*, 2013 UT 68, ¶ 130 n.23.

The rule addresses direct custodial questioning by law enforcement as well as other conduct during custodial questioning. It is intended to ensure that the custodial interrogation, including any part of the interrogation that is written or electronically transmitted, is fully and fairly recorded. Also, the admissibility of evidence under this rule is a preliminary question governed by Rule 104.'

Article VII Opinions And Expert Testimony

Rule 701. Opinion Testimony by Lay Witnesses

If a witness is not testifying as an expert, testimony in the form of an opinion is limited to one that is:

(a)   rationally based on the witness's perception;

(b)   helpful to clearly understanding the witness's testimony or to determining a fact in issue; and

(c)   not based on scientific, technical, or other specialized knowledge within the scope of Rule 702.

2011 Advisory Committee Note. – The language of this rule has been amended as part of the restyling of the Evidence Rules to make them more easily understood and to make style and terminology consistent throughout the rules. These changes are intended to be stylistic only. There is no intent to change any result in any ruling on evidence admissibility. This rule is the federal rule, verbatim.

Rule 702. Testimony by Experts

(a)   Subject to the limitations in paragraph (b), a witness who is qualified as an expert by knowledge, skill, experience, training, or education may testify in the form of an opinion or otherwise if the expert's scientific, technical, or other specialized knowledge will help the trier of fact to understand the evidence or to determine a fact in issue.

(b)   Scientific, technical, or other specialized knowledge may serve as the basis for expert testimony only if there is a threshold showing that the principles or methods that are underlying in the testimony

         (1) are reliable,

         (2) are based upon sufficient facts or data, and

         (3) have been reliably applied to the facts.

(c)   The threshold showing required by paragraph (b) is satisfied if the underlying principles or methods, including the sufficiency of facts or data and the manner of their application to the facts of the case, are generally accepted by the relevant expert community.

2011 Advisory Committee Note. – The language of this rule has been amended as part of the restyling of the Evidence Rules to make them more easily understood and to make style and terminology consistent throughout the rules. These changes are intended to be stylistic only. There is no intent to change any result in any ruling on evidence admissibility.

ADVISORY COMMITTEE NOTE.

Apart from its introductory clause, part (a) of the amended Rule recites verbatim Federal Rule 702 as it appeared before it was amended in 2000 to respond to Daubert v. Merrell Dow Pharmaceuticals, Inc., 509 U.S. 579 (1993). The 2007 amendment to the Rule added that introductory clause, along with parts (b) and (c). Unlike its predecessor, the amended rule does not incorporate the text of the Federal Rule. Although Utah law foreshadowed in many respects the developments in federal law that commenced with Daubert, the 2007 amendment preserves and clarifies differences between the Utah and federal approaches to expert testimony.

The amended rule embodies several general considerations. First, the rule is intended to be applied to all expert testimony. In this respect, the rule follows federal law as announced in Kumho Tire Co. v. Carmichael, 526 U.S. 137 (1999). Next, like its federal counterpart, Utah's rule assigns to trial judges a "gatekeeper" responsibility to screen out unreliable expert testimony. In performing their gatekeeper function, trial judges should confront proposed expert testimony with rational skepticism. This degree of scrutiny is not so rigorous as to be satisfied only by scientific or other specialized principles or methods that are free of controversy or that meet any fixed set of criteria fashioned to test reliability. The rational skeptic is receptive to any plausible evidence that may bear on reliability. She is mindful that several principles, methods or techniques may be suitably reliable to merit admission into evidence for consideration by the trier of fact. The fields of knowledge which may be drawn upon are not limited merely to the "scientific" and "technical", but extend to all "specialized" knowledge. Similarly, the expert is viewed, not in a narrow sense, but as a person qualified by "knowledge, skill, experience, training or education". Finally, the gatekeeping trial judge must take care to direct her skepticism to the particular proposition that the expert testimony is offered to support. The Daubert court characterized this task as focusing on the "work at hand". The practitioner should equally take care that the proffered expert testimony reliably addresses the "work at hand", and that the foundation of reliability presented for it reflects that consideration.

Section (c) retains limited features of the traditional Frye test for expert testimony. Generally accepted principles and methods may be admitted based on judicial notice. The nature of the "work at hand" is especially important here. It might be important in some cases for an expert to educate the factfinder about general principles, without attempting to apply these principles to the specific facts of the case. The rule recognizes that an expert on the stand may give a dissertation or exposition of principles relevant to the case, leaving the trier of fact to apply them to the facts. Proposed expert testimony that seeks to set out relevant principles, methods or techniques without offering an opinion about how they should be applied to a particular array of facts will be, in most instances, more eligible for admission under section (c) than case specific opinion testimony. There are, however, scientific or specialized methods or techniques applied at a level of considerable operational detail that have acquired sufficient general acceptance to merit admission under section (c).

The concept of general acceptance as used in section (c) is intended to replace the novel vs. non-novel dichotomy that has served as a central analytical tool in Utah's Rule 702 jurisprudence. The failure to show general acceptance meriting admission under section (c) does not mean the evidence is inadmissible, only that the threshold showing for reliability under section (b) must be shown by other means.

Section (b) adopts the three general categories of inquiry for expert testimony contained in the federal rule. Unlike the federal rule, however, the Utah rule notes that the proponent of the testimony is required to make only a "threshold" showing. That "threshold" requires only a basic foundational showing of indicia of reliability for the testimony to be admissible, not that the opinion is indisputably correct. When a trial court, applying this amendment, rules that an expert's testimony is reliable, this does not necessarily mean that contradictory expert testimony is unreliable. The amendment is broad enough to permit testimony that is the product of competing principles or methods in the same field of expertise. Contrary and inconsistent opinions may simultaneously meet the threshold; it is for the factfinder to reconcile - or choose between - the different opinions. As such, this amendment is not intended to provide an excuse for an automatic challenge to the testimony of every expert, and it is not contemplated that evidentiary hearings will be routinely required in order for the trial judge to fulfill his role as a rationally skeptical gatekeeper. In the typical case, admissibility under the rule may be determined based on affidavits, expert reports prepared pursuant to Utah R.Civ.P. 26, deposition testimony and memoranda of counsel.

Rule 703. Bases of an Expert's Opinion Testimony

An expert may base an opinion on facts or data in the case that the expert has been made aware of or personally observed. If experts in the particular field would reasonably rely on those kinds of facts or data in forming an opinion on the subject, they need not be admissible for the opinion to be admitted. But if the facts or data would otherwise be inadmissible, the proponent of the opinion may disclose them to the jury only if their probative value in helping the jury evaluate the opinion substantially outweighs their prejudicial effect.

2011 Advisory Committee Note. – The language of this rule has been amended as part of the restyling of the Evidence Rules to make them more easily understood and to make style and terminology consistent throughout the rules. These changes are intended to be stylistic only. There is no intent to change any result in any ruling on evidence admissibility. This rule is the federal rule, verbatim.

ADVISORY COMMITTEE NOTE

This rule is the federal rule, verbatim. The 2009 amendment adopts changes made to Federal Rule of Evidence 703 effective December 1, 2000.

Rule 704. Opinion on Ultimate Issue.

(a) **In General — Not Automatically Objectionable.** An opinion is not objectionable just because it embraces an ultimate issue.

(b) **Exception.** In a criminal case, an expert witness must not state an opinion about whether the defendant did or did not have a mental state or condition that constitutes an element of the crime charged or of a defense. Those matters are for the trier of fact alone.

2011 Advisory Committee Note. – The language of this rule has been amended as part of the restyling of the Evidence Rules to make them more easily understood and to make style and terminology consistent throughout the

rules. These changes are intended to be stylistic only. There is no intent to change any result in any ruling on evidence admissibility. This rule is the federal rule, verbatim.

ADVISORY COMMITTEE NOTE

This rule is the federal rule, verbatim, and comports with Rule 56(4), Utah Rules of Evidence (1971). See Edwards v. Didericksen, 597 P.2d 1328 (Utah 1979).

This rule is identical to Rule 704 of the Federal Rules of Evidence as amended in 1984.

Rule 705. Disclosing the Facts or Data Underlying an Expert's Opinion

Unless the court orders otherwise, an expert may state an opinion — and give the reasons for it — without first testifying to the underlying facts or data. But the expert may be required to disclose those facts or data on cross-examination.

2011 Advisory Committee Note. – The language of this rule has been amended as part of the restyling of the Evidence Rules to make them more easily understood and to make style and terminology consistent throughout the rules. These changes are intended to be stylistic only. There is no intent to change any result in any ruling on evidence admissibility. This rule is the federal rule, verbatim.

ADVISORY COMMITTEE NOTE

This rule is the federal rule, verbatim. The substance of this rule was formerly found in Rules 57 and 58, Utah Rules of Evidence (1971). The requirement that an expert disclose the underlying facts or data for his opinion when cross-examined was formerly found in Rule 58, Utah Rules of Evidence (1971). The discretion vested in the trial judge to require prior disclosure of underlying facts or data should be liberally exercised in situations where there has not been adequate discovery in civil cases or disclosure in criminal cases.

Rule 706. Court-Appointed Experts

(a) **Appointment Process**. On a party's motion or on its own, the court may order the parties to show cause why expert witnesses should not be appointed and may ask the parties to submit nominations. The court may appoint any expert that the parties agree on and any of its own choosing. But the court may only appoint someone who consents to act.

(b) **Expert's Role**. The court must inform the expert of the expert's duties. The court may do so in writing and have a copy filed with the clerk or may do so orally at a conference in which the parties have an opportunity to participate. The expert:

   (1) must advise the parties of any findings the expert makes;

   (2) may be deposed by any party;

   (3) may be called to testify by the court or any party; and

   (4) may be cross-examined by any party, including the party that called the expert.

(c) **Compensation**. The expert is entitled to a reasonable compensation, as set by the court. The compensation is payable as follows:

   (1) in a criminal case or in a civil case involving just compensation under the Fifth Amendment, from any funds that are provided by law; and

   (2) in any other civil case, by the parties in the proportion and at the time that the court directs — and the compensation is then charged like other costs.

2011 Advisory Committee Note. – The language of this rule has been amended as part of the restyling of the Evidence Rules to make them more easily understood and to make style and terminology consistent throughout the rules. These changes are intended to be stylistic only. There is no intent to change any result in any ruling on evidence admissibility. This rule is the federal rule, verbatim.

ADVISORY COMMITTEE NOTE

This rule is the federal rule, verbatim. Rules 59-61 of the Uniform Rules of Evidence (1953), on which the Utah Rules of Evidence (1971) were patterned, provided for the appointment, compensation and handling of appointed expert witness testimony. These rules were not adopted in the state of Utah. The reason for the rejection is unknown. However, the Utah Supreme Court has previously indicated that a trial judge has inherent authority to call a witness. Merchants Bank v. Goodfellow, 44 Utah 349, 140 P. 759 (1914).

Article VIII Hearsay

Rule 801. Definitions That Apply to This Article; Exclusions from Hearsay

(a) **Statement**. "Statement" means a person's oral assertion, written assertion, or nonverbal conduct, if the person intended it as an assertion.

(b) **Declarant**. "Declarant" means the person who made the statement.

(c) **Hearsay**. "Hearsay" means a statement that:

(1) the declarant does not make while testifying at the current trial or hearing; and

(2) a party offers in evidence to prove the truth of the matter asserted in the statement.

(d) **Statements That Are Not Hearsay**. A statement that meets the following conditions is not hearsay:

(1) **A Declarant-Witness's Prior Statement.** The declarant testifies and is subject to cross-examination about a prior statement, and the statement:

(A) is inconsistent with the declarant's testimony or the declarant denies having made the statement or has forgotten, or

(B) is consistent with the declarant's testimony and is offered to rebut an express or implied charge that the declarant recently fabricated it or acted from a recent improper influence or motive in so testifying; or

(C) identifies a person as someone the declarant perceived earlier.

(2) **An Opposing Party's Statement.** The statement is offered against an opposing party and:

(A) was made by the party in an individual or representative capacity;

(B) is one the party manifested that it adopted or believed to be true;

(C) was made by a person whom the party authorized to make a statement on the subject;

(D) was made by the party's agent or employee on a matter within the scope of that relationship and while it existed; or

(E) was made by the party's coconspirator during and in furtherance of the conspiracy.

2011 Advisory Committee Note. – The language of this rule has been amended as part of the restyling of the Evidence Rules to make them more easily understood and to make style and terminology consistent throughout the rules. These changes are intended to be stylistic only. There is no intent to change any result in any ruling on evidence admissibility.

ADVISORY COMMITTEE NOTE

Subsection (a) is in accord with Rule 62(1), Utah Rules of Evidence (1971).

Subsection (b) is in accord with Rule 62(2), Utah Rules of Evidence (1971). The hearsay rule is not applicable in declarations of devices and machines, e.g., radar. The definition of "hearsay" in subdivision (c) is substantially the same as Rule 63, Utah Rules of Evidence (1971).

Subdivision (d)(1) is similar to Rule 63(1), Utah Rules of Evidence (1971). It deviates from the federal rule in that it allows use of prior statements as substantive evidence if (1) inconsistent or (2) the witness has forgotten, and does not require the prior statement to have been given under oath or subject to perjury. The former Utah rules admitted such statements as an exception to the hearsay rule. See California v. Green, 399 U.S. 149 (1970), with respect to confrontation problems under the Sixth Amendment to the United States Constitution. Subdivision (d)(1) is as originally promulgated by the United States Supreme Court with the addition of the language "or the witness denies having made the statement or has forgotten" and is in keeping with the prior Utah rule and the actual effect on most juries.

Subdivision (d)(1)(B) is in substance the same as Rule 63(1), Utah Rules of Evidence (1971). The Utah court has been liberal in its interpretation of the applicable rule in this general area. State v. Sibert, 6 Utah 2d 198, 310 P.2d 388 (1957).

Subdivision (d)(1)(C) comports with prior Utah case law. State v. Owens, 15 Utah 2d 123, 388 P.2d 797 (1964); State v. Vasquez, 22 Utah 2d 277, 451 P.2d 786 (1969).

The substance of subdivision (d)(2)(A) was contained in Rules 63(6) and (7), Utah Rules of Evidence (1971), as an exception to the hearsay rule.

Similar provisions to subdivisions (d)(2)(B) and (C) were contained in Rule 63(8), Utah Rules of Evidence (1971), as an exception to the hearsay rule.

Rule 63(9), Utah Rules of Evidence (1971), was of similar substance and scope to subdivision (d)(2)(D), except that Rule 63(9) required that the declarant be unavailable before such admissions are received. Adoptive and vicarious admissions have been recognized as admissible in criminal as well as civil cases. State v. Kerekes, 622 P.2d 1161 (Utah 1980).

Statements by a coconspirator of a party made during the course and in furtherance of the conspiracy, admissible as non-hearsay under subdivision (d)(2)(E), have traditionally been admitted as exceptions to the hearsay rule. State v. Erwin, 101 Utah 365, 120 P.2d 285 (1941). Rule 63(9)(b), Utah Rules of Evidence (1971), was broader than this rule in that it provided for the admission of statements made while the party and declarant were participating in a plan to commit a crime or a civil wrong if the statement was relevant to the plan or its subject matter and made while the plan was in existence and before its complete execution or other termination.

Rule 802. The Rule Against Hearsay

Hearsay is not admissible except as provided by law or by these rules.

2011 Advisory Committee Note. – The language of this rule has been amended as part of the restyling of the Evidence Rules to make them more easily understood and to make style and terminology consistent throughout the rules. These changes are intended to be stylistic only. There is no intent to change any result in any ruling on evidence admissibility. This rule is the federal rule, verbatim.

ADVISORY COMMITTEE NOTE

This rule is Rule 802 of the Uniform Rules of Evidence (1974), and is the same as the first paragraph of Rule 63, Utah Rules of Evidence (1971).

Rule 803. Exceptions to the Rule Against Hearsay — Regardless of Whether the Declarant Is Available as a Witness

The following are not excluded by the rule against hearsay, regardless of whether the declarant is available as a witness:

  (1) **Present Sense Impression**. A statement describing or explaining an event or condition, made while or immediately after the declarant perceived it.

  (2) **Excited Utterance**. A statement relating to a startling event or condition, made while the declarant was under the stress of excitement that it caused.

  (3) **Then-Existing Mental, Emotional, or Physical Condition**. A statement of the declarant's then-existing state of mind (such as motive, intent, or plan) or emotional, sensory, or physical condition (such as mental feeling, pain, or bodily health), but not including a statement of memory or belief to prove the fact remembered or believed unless it relates to the validity or terms of the declarant's will.

  (4) **Statement Made for Medical Diagnosis or Treatment**. A statement that:

    (A) is made for — and is reasonably pertinent to — medical diagnosis or treatment; and

    (B) describes medical history; past or present symptoms or sensations; their inception; or their general cause.

  (5) **Recorded Recollection**. A record that:

(A) is on a matter the witness once knew about but now cannot recall well enough to testify fully and accurately;

(B) was made or adopted by the witness when the matter was fresh in the witness's memory; and

(C) accurately reflects the witness's knowledge.

If admitted, the record may be read into evidence but may be received as an exhibit only if offered by an adverse party.

(6) Records of a Regularly Conducted Activity. A record of an act, event, condition, opinion, or diagnosis if:

(A) the record was made at or near the time by — or from information transmitted by — someone with knowledge;

(B) the record was kept in the course of a regularly conducted activity of a business, organization, occupation, or calling, whether or not for profit;

(C) making the record was a regular practice of that activity;

(D) all these conditions are shown by the testimony of the custodian or another qualified witness, or by a certification that complies with Rule 902(11) or (12) or with a statute permitting certification; and

(E) neither the source of information nor the method or circumstances of preparation indicate a lack of trustworthiness.

(7) Absence of a Record of a Regularly Conducted Activity. Evidence that a matter is not included in a record described in paragraph (6) if:

(A) the evidence is admitted to prove that the matter did not occur or exist;

(B) a record was regularly kept for a matter of that kind; and

(C) neither the possible source of the information nor other circumstances indicate a lack of trustworthiness.

(8) Public Records. A record or statement of a public office if:

(A) it sets out:

(i) the office's activities;

(ii) a matter observed while under a legal duty to report, but not including, in a criminal case, a matter observed by law-enforcement personnel; or

(iii) in a civil case or against the government in a criminal case, factual findings from a legally authorized investigation; and

(B) neither the source of information nor other circumstances indicate a lack of trustworthiness.

(9) Public Records of Vital Statistics. A record of a birth, death, or marriage, if reported to a public office in accordance with a legal duty.

(10) Absence of a Public Record. Testimony — or a certification under Rule 902 — that a diligent search failed to disclose a public record or statement if the testimony or certification is admitted to prove that:

(A) the record or statement does not exist; or

(B) a matter did not occur or exist, if a public office regularly kept a record or statement for a matter of that kind.

(11) Records of Religious Organizations Concerning Personal or Family History. A statement of birth, legitimacy, ancestry, marriage, divorce, death, relationship by blood or marriage, or similar facts of personal or family history, contained in a regularly kept record of a religious organization.

(12) Certificates of Marriage, Baptism, and Similar Ceremonies. A statement of fact contained in a certificate:

(A) made by a person who is authorized by a religious organization or by law to perform the act certified;

(B) attesting that the person performed a marriage or similar ceremony or administered a sacrament; and

(C) purporting to have been issued at the time of the act or within a reasonable time after it.

(13) Family Records. A statement of fact about personal or family history contained in a family record, such as a Bible, genealogy, chart, engraving on a ring, inscription on a portrait, or engraving on an urn or burial marker.

(14) Records of Documents That Affect an Interest in Property. The record of a document that purports to establish or affect an interest in property if:

(A) the record is admitted to prove the content of the original recorded document, along with its signing and its delivery by each person who purports to have signed it;

(B) the record is kept in a public office; and

(C) a statute authorizes recording documents of that kind in that office.

(15) Statements in Documents That Affect an Interest in Property. A statement contained in a document that purports to establish or affect an interest in property if the matter stated was relevant to the document's purpose — unless later dealings with the property are inconsistent with the truth of the statement or the purport of the document.

(16) Statements in Ancient Documents. A statement in a document that is at least 20 years old and whose authenticity is established.

(17) Market Reports and Similar Commercial Publications. Market quotations, lists, directories, or other compilations that are generally relied on by the public or by persons in particular occupations.

(18) Statements in Learned Treatises, Periodicals, or Pamphlets. A statement contained in a treatise, periodical, or pamphlet if:

(A) the statement is called to the attention of an expert witness on cross-examination or relied on by the expert on direct examination; and

(B) the publication is established as a reliable authority by the expert's admission or testimony, by another expert's testimony, or by judicial notice.

If admitted, the statement may be read into evidence but not received as an exhibit.

(19) Reputation Concerning Personal or Family History. A reputation among a person's family by blood, adoption, or marriage — or among a person's associates or in the community — concerning the person's birth, adoption, legitimacy, ancestry, marriage, divorce, death, relationship by blood, adoption, or marriage, or similar facts of personal or family history.

(20) Reputation Concerning Boundaries or General History. A reputation in a community — arising before the controversy — concerning boundaries of land in the community or customs that affect the land, or concerning general historical events important to that community, state, or nation.

(21) Reputation Concerning Character. A reputation among a person's associates or in the community concerning the person's character.

(22) Judgment of a Previous Conviction. Evidence of a final judgment of conviction if:

    (A) the judgment was entered after a trial or guilty plea, but not a nolo contendere plea;

    (B) the conviction was for a crime punishable by death or by imprisonment for more than a year;

    (C) the evidence is admitted to prove any fact essential to the judgment; and

    (D) when offered by the prosecutor in a criminal case for a purpose other than impeachment, the judgment was against the defendant.

The pendency of an appeal may be shown but does not affect admissibility.

(23) Judgments Involving Personal, Family, or General History or a Boundary. A judgment that is admitted to prove a matter of personal, family, or general history, or boundaries, if the matter:

    (A) was essential to the judgment; and

    (B) could be proved by evidence of reputation.

(24) *[Other exceptions.]* [Transferred to Rule 807.]

2011 Advisory Committee Note. – The language of this rule has been amended as part of the restyling of the Evidence Rules to make them more easily understood and to make style and terminology consistent throughout the

rules. These changes are intended to be stylistic only. There is no intent to change any result in any ruling on evidence admissibility. This rule is the federal rule, verbatim.

ADVISORY COMMITTEE NOTE

This rule is the federal rule verbatim. The 2001 amendment adopts changes made to Federal Rule of Evidence 803(6) effective December 1, 2000.

Rule 804. Exceptions to the Rule Against Hearsay – When the Declarant is Unavailable as a Witness

(a) **Criteria for Being Unavailable**. A declarant is considered to be unavailable as a witness if the declarant:

(1) is exempted from testifying about the subject matter of the declarant's statement because the court rules that a privilege applies;

(2) refuses to testify about the subject matter despite a court order to do so;

(3) testifies to not remembering the subject matter;

(4) cannot be present or testify at the trial or hearing because of death or a then-existing infirmity, physical illness, or mental illness; or

(5) is absent from the trial or hearing and the statement's proponent has not been able, by process or other reasonable means, to procure the declarant'sattendance.

But this subdivision (a) does not apply if the statement's proponent procured or wrongfully caused the declarant's unavailability as a witness in order to prevent the declarant from attending or testifying.

(b) **The Exceptions**. The following are not excluded by the rule against hearsay if the declarant is unavailable as a witness:

(1) **Former Testimony. Testimony that:**

    (A) was given as a witness at a trial, hearing, or lawful deposition, whether given during the current proceeding or a different one; and

    (B) is now offered against a party who had — or, in a civil case, whose predecessor in interest had — an opportunity and similar motive to develop it by direct, cross-, or redirect examination.

(2) **Statement Under the Belief of Imminent Death.** In a civil or criminal case, a statement made by the declarant while believing the declarant's death to be imminent, if the judge finds it was made in good faith.

(3) **Statement Against Interest.** A statement that:

    (A) a reasonable person in the declarant's position would have made only if the person believed it to be true because, when made, it was so contrary to the declarant's proprietary or pecuniary interest or had so great a tendency to invalidate the declarant's claim against someone else or to expose the declarant to civil or criminal liability; and

    (B) is supported by corroborating circumstances that clearly indicate its trustworthiness, if it is offered in a criminal case as one that tends to expose the declarant to criminal liability.

(4) **Statement of Personal or Family History.** A statement about:

    (A) the declarant's own birth, adoption, legitimacy, ancestry, marriage, divorce, relationship by blood or marriage, or similar facts of personal or family history, even though the declarant had no way of acquiring personal knowledge about that fact; or

(B) another person concerning any of these facts, as well as death, if the declarant was related to the person by blood, adoption, or marriage or was so intimately associated with the person's family that the declarant's information is likely to be accurate.

2011 Advisory Committee Note. – The language of this rule has been amended as part of the restyling of the Evidence Rules to make them more easily understood and to make style and terminology consistent throughout the rules. These changes are intended to be stylistic only. There is no intent to change any result in any ruling on evidence admissibility.

ADVISORY COMMITTEE NOTE

Subdivision (a) is comparable to Rule 63(7), Utah Rules of Evidence (1971). Rule 62(7)[(e)], Utah Rules of Evidence (1971), seems to be encompassed in Rule 804(a)(5). Subdivision (a)(5) is a modification of the federal rule which permits judicial discretion to be applied in determining unavailability of a witness.

Subdivision (b)(1) is comparable to Rule 63(3), Utah Rules of Evidence (1971), but the former rule is broader to the extent that it did not limit the admission of the testimony to a situation where the party to the action had the interest and opportunity to develop the testimony. Condas v. Condas, 618 P.2d 491 (Utah 1980); State v. Brooks, 638 P.2d 537 (Utah 1981).

Subdivision (b)(2) is comparable to Rule 63(5), Utah Rules of Evidence (1971), but the former rule was not limited to declarations concerning the cause or circumstances of the impending death nor did it limit dying declarations in criminal prosecutions to homicide cases. The rule has been modified by making it applicable to any civil or criminal proceeding, subject to the qualification that the judge finds the statement to have been made in good faith.

Subdivision (b)(3) is comparable to Rule 63(10), Utah Rules of Evidence (1971), though it does not extend merely to social interests.

Subdivision (b)(4) is similar to Rule 63(24), Utah Rules of Evidence (1971).

Subdivision (b)(5) had no counterpart in Utah Rules of Evidence (1971).

Rule 805. Hearsay Within Hearsay

Hearsay within hearsay is not excluded by the rule against hearsay if each part of the combined statements conforms with an exception to the rule.

2011 Advisory Committee Note. – The language of this rule has been amended as part of the restyling of the Evidence Rules to make them more easily understood and to make style and terminology consistent throughout the rules. These changes are intended to be stylistic only. There is no intent to change any result in any ruling on evidence admissibility. This rule is the federal rule, verbatim.

ADVISORY COMMITTEE NOTE

This rule is the federal rule, verbatim. A similar provision was contained in Rule 66, Utah Rules of Evidence (1971).

Rule 806. Attacking and Supporting the Declarant's Credibility

When a hearsay statement — or a statement described in Rule 801(d)(2)(C), (D), or (E) — has been admitted in evidence, the declarant's credibility may be attacked, and then supported, by any evidence that would be admissible for those purposes if the declarant had testified as a witness. The court may admit evidence of the declarant's inconsistent statement or conduct, regardless of when it occurred or whether the declarant had an opportunity to explain or deny it. If the party against whom the statement was admitted calls the declarant as a witness, the party may examine the declarant on the statement as if on cross-examination.

2011 Advisory Committee Note. – The language of this rule has been amended as part of the restyling of the Evidence Rules to make them more easily understood and to make style and terminology consistent throughout the rules. These changes are intended to be stylistic only. There is no intent to change any result in any ruling on evidence admissibility. This rule is the federal rule, verbatim.

ADVISORY COMMITTEE NOTE

This rule is the federal rule, verbatim. Rule 65, Utah Rules of Evidence (1971), contained a comparable provision.

Rule 807. Residual Exception

(a) **In General**. Under the following circumstances, a hearsay statement is not excluded by the rule against hearsay even if the statement is not specifically covered by a hearsay exception in Rule 803 or 804:

(1) the statement has equivalent circumstantial guarantees of trustworthiness;

(2) it is offered as evidence of a material fact;

(3) it is more probative on the point for which it is offered than any other evidence that the proponent can obtain through reasonable efforts; and

(4) admitting it will best serve the purposes of these rules and the interests of justice.

(b) **Notice**. The statement is admissible only if, before the trial or hearing, the proponent gives an adverse party reasonable notice of the intent to offer the statement and its particulars, including the declarant's name and address, so that the party has a fair opportunity to meet it.

2011 Advisory Committee Note. – The language of this rule has been amended as part of the restyling of the Evidence Rules to make them more easily understood and to make style and terminology consistent throughout the rules. These changes are intended to be stylistic only. There is no intent to change any result in any ruling on evidence admissibility. This rule is the federal rule, verbatim.

ADVISORY COMMITTEE NOTE

This rule transfers identical provisions Rule 803(24) and Rule 804(b)(5) to a new Rule 807 to reflect the organization found in the Federal Rules of Evidence. No substantive change is intended. This rule is the federal rule, verbatim.

Article IX Authentication And Identification

Rule 901. Authenticating or Identifying Evidence

(a)   **In General**. To satisfy the requirement of authenticating or identifying an item of evidence, the proponent must produce evidence sufficient to support a finding that the item is what the proponent claims it is.

(b)   **Examples**. The following are examples only — not a complete list — of evidence that satisfies the requirement:

(1)   **Testimony of a Witness with Knowledge**. Testimony that an item is what it is claimed to be.

(2)   **Nonexpert Opinion About Handwriting**. A nonexpert's opinion that handwriting is genuine, based on a familiarity with it that was not acquired for the current litigation.

(3)   **Comparison by an Expert Witness or the Trier of Fact**. A comparison with an authenticated specimen by an expert witness or the trier of fact.

(4) Distinctive Characteristics and the Like. The appearance, contents, substance, internal patterns, or other distinctive characteristics of the item, taken together with all the circumstances.

(5) Opinion About a Voice. An opinion identifying a person's voice — whether heard firsthand or through mechanical or electronic transmission or recording — based on hearing the voice at any time under circumstances that connect it with the alleged speaker.

(6) Evidence About a Telephone Conversation. For a telephone conversation, evidence that a call was made to the number assigned at the time to:

(A) a particular person, if circumstances, including self-identification, show that the person answering was the one called; or

(B) a particular business, if the call was made to a business and the call related to business reasonably transacted over the telephone.

(7) Evidence About Public Records. Evidence that:

(A) a document was recorded or filed in a public office as authorized by law; or

(B) a purported public record or statement is from the office where items of this kind are kept.

(8) Evidence About Ancient Documents or Data Compilations. For a document or data compilation, evidence that it:

(A) is in a condition that creates no suspicion about its authenticity;

(B) was in a place where, if authentic, it would likely be; and

(C) is at least 20 years old when offered.

(9) Evidence About a Process or System. Evidence describing a process or system and showing that it produces an accurate result.

(10) Methods Provided by a Statute or Rule. Any method of authentication or identification allowed by court rule or statute of this state.

2011 Advisory Committee Note. – The language of this rule has been amended as part of the restyling of the Evidence Rules to make them more easily understood and to make style and terminology consistent throughout the rules. These changes are intended to be stylistic only. There is no intent to change any result in any ruling on evidence admissibility. This rule is the federal rule, verbatim.

ADVISORY COMMITTEE NOTE

Subdivision (b)(2) is in accord with State v. Freshwater, 30 Utah 442, 85 Pac. 447 (1906). Subdivision (b)(8) is comparable with Rule 67, Utah Rules of Evidence (1971), except that the former rule imposed a 30-year requirement. Subdivision (b)(10) is an adaptation of subdivision (10) in the comparable federal rules to conform to state practice.

Rule 902. Evidence That Is Self-Authenticating

The following items of evidence are self-authenticating; they require no extrinsic evidence of authenticity in order to be admitted:

(1) Domestic Public Documents That Are Sealed and Signed. A document that bears:

    (A) a seal purporting to be that of the United States; any state, district, commonwealth, territory, or insular possession of the United States; the former Panama Canal Zone; the Trust Territory of the Pacific Islands; a political subdivision of any of these entities; or a department, agency, or officer of any entity named above; and

(B) a signature purporting to be an execution or attestation.

(2) **Domestic Public Documents That Are Not Sealed But Are Signed and Certified**. A document that bears no seal if:

(A) it bears the signature of an officer or employee of an entity named in Rule 902(1)(A); and

(B) another public officer who has a seal and official duties within that same entity certifies under seal — or its equivalent — that the signer has the official capacity and that the signature is genuine.

(3) **Foreign Public Documents**. A document that purports to be signed or attested by a person who is authorized by a foreign country's law to do so. The document must be accompanied by a final certification that certifies the genuineness of the signature and official position of the signer or attester — or of any foreign official whose certificate of genuineness relates to the signature or attestation or is in a chain of certificates of genuineness relating to the signature or attestation. The certification may be made by a secretary of a United States embassy or legation; by a consul general, vice consul, or consular agent of the United States; or by a diplomatic or consular official of the foreign country assigned or accredited to the United States. If all parties have been given a reasonable opportunity to investigate the document's authenticity and accuracy, the court may, for good cause, either:

(A) order that it be treated as presumptively authentic without final certification; or

(B) allow it to be evidenced by an attested summary with or without final certification.

(4) **Certified Copies of Public Records**. A copy of an official record — or a copy of a document that was recorded or filed in a public office as authorized by law — if the copy is certified as correct by:

(A) the custodian or another person authorized to make the certification; or

(B) a certificate that complies with Rule 902(1), (2), or (3), or any law of the United States or of this state.

(5) Official publications. Books, pamphlet, or other publication purporting to be issued by public authority.

(6) Newspapers and Periodicals. Printed material purporting to be a newspaper or periodical.

(7) Trade Inscriptions and the Like. An inscription, sign, tag, or label purporting to have been affixed in the course of business and indicating origin, ownership, or control.

(8) Acknowledged Documents. A document accompanied by a certificate of acknowledgment that is lawfully executed by a notary public or another officer who is authorized to take acknowledgments.

(9) Commercial Paper and Related Documents. Commercial paper, a signature on it, and related documents, to the extent allowed by general commercial law.

(10) Presumptions Under a Federal Statute. A signature, document, or anything else that a federal statute declares to be presumptively or prima facie genuine or authentic.

(11) Certified Domestic Records of a Regularly Conducted Activity. The original or a copy of a domestic record that meets the requirements of Rule 803(6)(A)-(C), as shown by a certification of the custodian or another qualified person that must be signed in a manner that, if falsely made, would subject the signer to criminal penalty under the laws where the certification was signed. Before the trial or hearing, the proponent must give an adverse party reasonable written notice of the intent to offer the record — and must make the record and certification available for inspection — so that the party has a fair opportunity to challenge them.

(12) Certified Foreign Records of a Regularly Conducted Activity. The original or a copy of a foreign

record that meets the requirements of Rule 803(6)(A)-(C), as shown by a certification of the custodian or

another qualified person that must be signed in a manner that, if falsely made, would subject the signer

to criminal penalty under the laws where the certification was signed. Before the trial or hearing, the

proponent must give an adverse party reasonable written notice of the intent to offer the record — and

must make the record and certification available for inspection — so that the party has a fair opportunity

to challenge them.

2011 Advisory Committee Note. – The language of this rule has been amended as part of the restyling of the

Evidence Rules to make them more easily understood and to make style and terminology consistent throughout the

rules. These changes are intended to be stylistic only. There is no intent to change any result in any ruling on

evidence admissibility. This rule is the federal rule, verbatim.

ADVISORY COMMITTEE NOTE

The amendment to Rule 803(6) and the addition of Rules 902(11) and 902(12) were made to track the changes made

to Federal Rule of Evidence 803(6) and the adoption of Federal Rules 902(11) and 902(12), effective December 1,

2000. The changes to the federal rules benefit from a federal statute allowing the use of declarations without

notarization. Utah has no comparable statute, so the requirements for declarations used under the rule are included

within the rule itself.

Rule 903. Subscribing Witness's Testimony

A subscribing witness's testimony is necessary to authenticate a writing only if required by the law of the jurisdiction

that governs its validity.

2011 Advisory Committee Note. – The language of this rule has been amended as part of the restyling of the Evidence Rules to make them more easily understood and to make style and terminology consistent throughout the rules. These changes are intended to be stylistic only. There is no intent to change any result in any ruling on evidence admissibility. This rule is the federal rule, verbatim.

ADVISORY COMMITTEE NOTE

This rule is the federal rule, verbatim. Statutory provisions concerning authentication of documents, such as, e.g., Title 78 Chapter 25, Utah Code Annotated (1953), are unchanged by this rule.

Article X Contents Of Writings, Recordings, And Photographs

Rule 1001. Definitions That Apply to This Article

In this article:

(a)	A "writing" consists of letters, words, numbers, or their equivalent set down in any form.

(b)	A "recording" consists of letters, words, numbers, or their equivalent recorded in any manner.

(c)	A "photograph" means a photographic image or its equivalent stored in any form.

(d)	An "original" of a writing or recording means the writing or recording itself or any counterpart intended to have the same effect by the person who executed or issued it. For electronically stored information, "original" means any printout — or other output readable by sight — if it accurately reflects the information. An "original" of a photograph includes the negative or a print from it.

(e)   A "duplicate" means a counterpart produced by a mechanical, photographic, chemical, electronic, or other equivalent process or technique that accurately reproduces the original.

2011 Advisory Committee Note. – The language of this rule has been amended as part of the restyling of the Evidence Rules to make them more easily understood and to make style and terminology consistent throughout the rules. These changes are intended to be stylistic only. There is no intent to change any result in any ruling on evidence admissibility. This rule is the federal rule, verbatim.

ADVISORY COMMITTEE NOTE

This rule is the federal rule, verbatim. The definition of "writing" in subdivision (1) corresponds in substance with Rule 1(12), Utah Rules of Evidence (1971).

Rule 1002. Requirement of the Original

An original writing, recording, or photograph is required in order to prove its content, except as otherwise provided in these rules or by other rules adopted by the Supreme Court of this State or by statute.

2011 Advisory Committee Note. – The language of this rule has been amended as part of the restyling of the Evidence Rules to make them more easily understood and to make style and terminology consistent throughout the rules. These changes are intended to be stylistic only. There is no intent to change any result in any ruling on evidence admissibility. This rule is the federal rule, verbatim.

ADVISORY COMMITTEE NOTE

This rule is Rule 1002, Uniform Rules of Evidence (1974).

Rule 1003. Admissibility of Duplicates

A duplicate is admissible to the same extent as the original unless a genuine question is raised about the original's authenticity or the circumstances make it unfair to admit the duplicate.

2011 Advisory Committee Note. – The language of this rule has been amended as part of the restyling of the Evidence Rules to make them more easily understood and to make style and terminology consistent throughout the rules. These changes are intended to be stylistic only. There is no intent to change any result in any ruling on evidence admissibility. This rule is the federal rule, verbatim.

ADVISORY COMMITTEE NOTE

This rule is the federal rule, verbatim, and is comparable to Rule 72, Utah Rules of Evidence (1971), but is broader than Rule 72 and the best evidence provisions of Rule 70, Utah Rules of Evidence (1971).

Rule 1004. Admissibility of Other Evidence of Content

An original is not required and other evidence of the content of a writing, recording, or photograph is admissible if:

(a) all the originals are lost or destroyed, and not by the proponent acting in bad faith;

(b) an original cannot be obtained by any available judicial process;

(c) the party against whom the original would be offered had control of the original; was at that time put on notice, by pleadings or otherwise, that the original would be a subject of proof at the trial or hearing; and fails to produce it at the trial or hearing; or

(d) the writing, recording, or photograph is not closely related to a controlling issue.

2011 Advisory Committee Note. – The language of this rule has been amended as part of the restyling of the Evidence Rules to make them more easily understood and to make style and terminology consistent throughout the rules. These changes are intended to be stylistic only. There is no intent to change any result in any ruling on evidence admissibility. This rule is the federal rule, verbatim.

ADVISORY COMMITTEE NOTE

This rule is the federal rule, verbatim, and embodies in a more comprehensive fashion the provisions of Rule 70, Utah Rules of Evidence (1971).

Rule 1005. Copies of Public Records to Prove Content

The proponent may use a copy to prove the content of an official record — or of a document that was recorded or filed in a public office as authorized by law — if these conditions are met: the record or document is otherwise admissible; and the copy is certified as correct in accordance with Rule 902(4) or is testified to be correct by a witness who has compared it with the original. If no such copy can be obtained by reasonable diligence, then the proponent may use other evidence to prove the content.

2011 Advisory Committee Note. – The language of this rule has been amended as part of the restyling of the Evidence Rules to make them more easily understood and to make style and terminology consistent throughout the

rules. These changes are intended to be stylistic only. There is no intent to change any result in any ruling on evidence admissibility. This rule is the federal rule, verbatim.

ADVISORY COMMITTEE NOTE

This rule is the federal rule, verbatim, and comports with the substance of Rule 68, Utah Rules of Evidence (1971).

Rule 1006. Summaries to Prove Content

The proponent may use a summary, chart, or calculation to prove the content of voluminous writings, recordings, or photographs that cannot be conveniently examined in court. The proponent must make the originals or duplicates available for examination or copying, or both, by other parties at a reasonable time or place. And the court may order the proponent to produce them in court.

2011 Advisory Committee Note. – The language of this rule has been amended as part of the restyling of the Evidence Rules to make them more easily understood and to make style and terminology consistent throughout the rules. These changes are intended to be stylistic only. There is no intent to change any result in any ruling on evidence admissibility. This rule is the federal rule, verbatim.

ADVISORY COMMITTEE NOTE

This rule is the federal rule, verbatim, and is comparable to the substance of Rule 70(f), Utah Rules of Evidence (1971).

Rule 1007. Testimony or Statement of a Party to Prove Content

The proponent may prove the content of a writing, recording, or photograph by the testimony, deposition, or written statement of the party against whom the evidence is offered. The proponent need not account for the original.

2011 Advisory Committee Note. – The language of this rule has been amended as part of the restyling of the Evidence Rules to make them more easily understood and to make style and terminology consistent throughout the rules. These changes are intended to be stylistic only. There is no intent to change any result in any ruling on evidence admissibility. This rule is the federal rule, verbatim.

ADVISORY COMMITTEE NOTE

This rule is the federal rule, verbatim. There was no comparable rule in the Utah Rules of Evidence (1971), but the rule appears to be in accord with Utah practice.

Rule 1008. Functions of the Court and Jury

Ordinarily, the court determines whether the proponent has fulfilled the factual conditions for admitting other evidence of the content of a writing, recording, or photograph under Rule 1004 or 1005. But in a jury trial, the jury determines — in accordance with Rule 104(b) — any issue about whether:

(a)   an asserted writing, recording, or photograph ever existed;

(b)   another one produced at the trial or hearing is the original; or

(c)   other evidence of content accurately reflects the content.

2011 Advisory Committee Note. – The language of this rule has been amended as part of the restyling of the Evidence Rules to make them more easily understood and to make style and terminology consistent throughout the

rules. These changes are intended to be stylistic only. There is no intent to change any result in any ruling on evidence admissibility. This rule is the federal rule, verbatim.

Article XI Miscellaneous Rules

Rule 1101. Applicability of Rules

(a)   **Proceedings Generally**. These rules apply to all actions and proceedings in the courts of this state except as otherwise provided in Subdivisions (c) and (d). They apply generally to civil actions and proceedings, criminal cases and contempt proceedings except those in which the court may act summarily.

(b)   **Rule of Privilege**. The rule with respect to privileges applies at all stages of all actions, cases and proceedings.

(c)   **Rules Inapplicable**. The rules (other than with respect to privileges) do not apply in the following situations:

(1)   **Preliminary Questions of Fact.** The determination of questions of fact preliminary to admissibility of evidence when the issue is to be determined by the court under rule 104.

(2)   **Grand Jury.** Proceedings before grand juries.

(3)   **Miscellaneous Proceedings.** Proceedings for extradition or rendition; sentencing, or granting or revoking probation; issuance of warrants for arrest, criminal summonses, and search warrants; and proceedings with respect to release on bail or otherwise.

(d)   **Reliable Hearsay in Criminal Preliminary Examinations**. In a criminal preliminary examination, reliable hearsay shall be admissible as provided under Rule 1102.

2011 Advisory Committee Note. – The language of this rule has been amended as part of the restyling of the Evidence Rules to make them more easily understood and to make style and terminology consistent throughout the rules. These changes are intended to be stylistic only. There is no intent to change any result in any ruling on evidence admissibility.

ADVISORY COMMITTEE NOTE

This rule is the federal rule, verbatim, and is substantially the same as Rule 70(2), Utah Rules of Evidence (1971).

Rule 1102. Reliable Hearsay in Criminal Preliminary Examinations

(a)   Statement of the Rule. Reliable hearsay is admissible at criminal preliminary examinations.

(b)   Definition of Reliable Hearsay. For purposes of criminal preliminary examinations only, reliable hearsay includes:

   (1)   hearsay evidence admissible at trial under the Utah Rules of Evidence;

   (2)   hearsay evidence admissible at trial under Rule 804 of the Utah Rules of Evidence, regardless of the availability of the declarant at the preliminary examination;

   (3)   evidence establishing the foundation for or the authenticity of any exhibit;

   (4)   scientific, laboratory, or forensic reports and records;

   (5)   medical and autopsy reports and records;

   (6)   a statement of a non-testifying peace officer to a testifying peace officer;

   (7)   a statement made by a child victim of physical abuse or a sexual offense which is recorded in accordance with Rule 15.5 of the Utah Rules of Criminal Procedure;

   (8)   a statement of a declarant that is written, recorded, or transcribed verbatim which is:

      (A)   under oath or affirmation; or

         (B)   pursuant to a notification to the declarant that a false statement made therein is punishable; and

   (9)   other hearsay evidence with similar indicia of reliability, regardless of admissibility at trial under Rules 803 and 804 of the Utah Rules of Evidence.

(c)   Continuance for Production of Additional Evidence. If hearsay evidence is proffered or admitted in the preliminary examination, a continuance of the hearing may be granted for the purpose of furnishing additional evidence if:

(1)   The magistrate finds that the hearsay evidence proffered or admitted is not sufficient and additional evidence is necessary for a bindover; or

(2)   The defense establishes that it would be so substantially and unfairly disadvantaged by the use of the hearsay evidence as to outweigh the interests of the declarant and the efficient administration of justice.

Effective December 1, 2017

2017 Advisory Committee Note. – The prompt reporting language in (b)(7) was removed.

Rule 1103. Title

These rules may be known and cited as the Utah Rules of Evidence.

Made in the USA
San Bernardino,
CA